EVERYMAN'S PRINCE

A Guide
to Understanding
Your Political
Problems

EVERYMAN'S PRINCE

A Guide
to Understanding
Your Political
Problems

Revised Edition

William D. Coplin and Michael K. O'Leary
Syracuse University

with the assistance of
John Vasquez and Karen Johnson

 Duxbury Press　　　　　　North Scituate, Massachusetts

Duxbury Press

A Division of Wadsworth Publishing Company, Inc.

EVERYMAN'S PRINCE: A Guide to Understanding Your Political Problems, revised edition, was edited and prepared for composition by Sylvia Stein. Interior design was provided by Dorothy Thompson, and the cover was designed by Dick Hannus.

L. C. Cat. Card No.: 75-43080
ISBN 0-87872-109-6
Printed in the United States of America

2 3 4 5 6 7 8 9 - 80 79 78 77

Contents

Section 3   THE CULMINATION

Preface

Underlying the ideas in this book are the following beliefs:

—Everyman has the capability and right to be a Prince, that is, to be a political actor rather than merely a political subject.

—Unless Everyman develops that capability and exercises that right he cannot realize himself by making the institutions surrounding him responsive to his needs.

—A society and government that reserves political awareness for its leaders precludes sustained adaptation to the complexities and challenges that threaten its existence.

—Political reason in the hands of no one leads to chaos, in the hands of a few leads to tyranny, in the hands of a moderate number of elites leads to stagnation, in the hands of Everyman leads ultimately to justice.

—The effective organization of modern society will not occur when the master plans of ideologists are realized but when *Everyman is a Prince*.

Much of our description of the political accounting system is carried out by suggesting its hypothetical application in many different situations. Some of the situations we use, such as the American Constitutional Convention and the career of Ralph Nader are based on fact; some are wholly imaginary. But in all cases we have taken poetic license in attributing actions, motivations, and particular modes of thought to the people we describe. We hope the illustrations will be read in this spirit.

As a final word, we make use of a fictitious organization, the PRINCEtitute, Inc., to suggest several possible applications (and misapplications) of the PRINCE political accounting system. No such organization as PRINCEtitute, Inc. exists, to our knowledge, nor has any organization ever carried on in quite the ways we have described. However, an organization called PRINCE Analysis, Inc. does exist and has developed a variety of PRINCE-based materials for political action and education.

Acknowledgement to the First Edition

We wish to thank the many readers of this manuscript and users of the political accounting system that it describes for their helpful comments and criticisms. In many cases their responses have induced us to shift our issue positions. We especially want to mention David Ahola and his students at Mohawk Valley Community College and Bernard Hennessy and his students at California State College-Hayward, as well as Theodore Becker, Robert Craig, Roger Davidson, Paul Goodwin, Harold Quinley, and Harmon Zeigler.

We also want to record our debts to two people especially important in helping us. John Vasquez collaborated in the formulation of the book, performed many essential research tasks, and contributed many of his own ideas. In addition, his firm belief in the book served to spur us on even when our faith faltered. Stephen L. Mills is a collaborator with us in the development of PRINCE, a programmed international computer environment. Our joint work in the development of that model has led us to focus on the basic concepts used in the PRINCE Political Accounting System. Without that effort, *Everyman's PRINCE* would not have been written.

A number of other individuals have been crucial in the development of the book because they have read and commented on one or more chapters. They include our wives, Merry and Linda; our "creative typist," Gloria Tripolone; and our colleagues at Syracuse, Robert McClure, Patrick McGowan, John Handelman, Howard Shapiro, and J. Martin Rochester.

Acknowledgment to the Revised Edition

A number of our colleagues at other institutions have used *Everyman's PRINCE* in their classrooms and passed on their own and their classes' reactions to us. We wish to thank each of them and to say that we hope this edition incorporates their suggestions. In particular, we want to thank A. Robert Thoeny (Memphis State University), Stephen A. Douglas (University of Illinois—Urbana), Jonathan Wilkenfeld (University of Maryland), and J. K. Morrison (University of Utah), who undertook pre-revision reviews of the earlier edition for the publisher.

We also want to thank Karen Johnson, who was in charge of revising this edition. In addition to making the routine changes required for the update, Karen wrote and revised various portions of the new text. She remained in good spirits throughout, which attests more to her personality than to the task and people she was working with.

Instructor's Introduction

Everyman's PRINCE is a lively attempt to translate the fruits of an ongoing research project about politics to a wide audience, including college students. In educating the reader in the essential characteristics of politics, it does not rely upon theoretical concepts, empirically testable hypotheses, and synthesis with the existing scholarly literature. Instead, it employs a "political accounting system" that all of us can use in understanding the political probelms we might encounter. Consisting of four simple charts built around four basic concepts the PRINCE political accounting system provides a policy analysis model.

After the brief description of the purpose of the book and the model in the first two chapters, the student is provided with examples of how the accounting system has been or might be used. Employing literary license, the authors analyze some well-known events and people—the Constitutional Convention, George Washington, and Ralph Nader—as if those in the political spotlight had used or misused the PRINCE political accounting system. Other chapters show how PRINCE can be used by a citizen trying to get his taxes reduced, an individual trying to get a traffic light installed on his neighborhood corner, a PRINCEtitute, Inc. case study of widgit-exporting countries, and an analysis of American economic policy.

We have also initiated in this edition a PRINCE-replay chapter based on the personal account of real political actors in real situations. Neal Bellos describes how he used the logic of the PRINCE system before its actual publication to get the Neighborhood Health Center approved in a midwestern city. The PRINCE-replay chapter provides students with the actual experiences of a political actor and serves as a model for them to become their own Prince.

The final section of the book provides information on the uses of the PRINCE accounting system as well as instructions for using a board game, PRINCEdown, and a computer simulation, PROBE, both of which build on PRINCE concepts. The information on PRINCEdown in Chapter 13 can be used to play and analyze the game if the instructor can acquire the requisite number of properly colored poker chips (sixty red and eighteen each of the other colors). The board for the game is illustrated right in the book and can be copied to play the game. An instructor who wishes to buy cardboard renditions of the board or a set of the chips should write to one of the authors. Either would be happy to sell the necessary material at cost (approximately $4.00).

PROBE involves a computer program that exists in interactive and batch language on computer cards. A set of the deck can be purchased from the International Relations Program of Syracuse University for $50.00. We have found that it runs on most computers that have relatively small, at least 8k, storage.

Thanks to a recent grant from the EXXON Education Foundation, we have been able to test the impact of the book, PRINCEdown, and PROBE on undergraduates. A paper* reports the results of the test, which appears on pages xii–xiv. You may wish to use the test also. Note that it is based on identifying the issues and a political strategy for a situation reported in the *New York Times*. In general, we have found it very useful to have students conduct various kinds of PRINCE analyses from the newspaper. The ability to read the newspaper and to identify issues and strategies is, we consider, an essential skill for every citizen. Our findings show that students who are exposed to PRINCE materials increase their ability to define political issues and identify political strategies in a pre/post evaluation. We also discovered, as might be expected, that the longer the exposure to the material and the more types of materials used (the book, PRINCEdown, PROBE), the more the gains between the pre and post tests.

Although the pedagogical aims of this book preclude scholarly references, the concepts and theories represented in it have a long scholarly pedigree. They follow the intellectual heritage of Bentley, Truman, and Dahl in political science. Recent work by the authors under a grant from the Social Science Division of the National Science Foundation has allowed us to formulate and test the concepts contained in this book under the general framework of reference group theory. Further information on this work can be obtained from the authors.

*Lawrence Bloom, William D. Coplin, and Michael K. O'Leary, "An Evaluation of PRINCE Materials for Teaching Skill in General Political Strategy" in *Teaching Political Science* (In Press).

S.U.N.Y. Chief Asks Tenure Analysis

By IVER PETERSON

State University Chancellor Ernest L. Boyer directed the 29 state-run campuses yesterday to "clarify" their standards for awarding tenure and to analyze their projected rate of granting such life-long faculty job security in the next six years.

Coming at a time when enrollment on S.U.N.Y. campuses is leveling off and new faculty employment opportunities are correspondingly diminished, the Chancellor's directive was seen as a cautious move to initiate discussion of tenure reform.

In his policy statement, he proposed lowering of the mandatory retirement age of faculty members from 70 to 65, and called for a program to reassign teachers in underenrolled subjects to "other, related academic fields."

The Chancellor's policy statement appeared to make an oblique reference to the controversial decision by the City University to limit the number of faculty members who may receive tenure. He asserted that "a rigid tenure quota system is unacceptable" for the S.U.N.Y. system.

Walking a Tightrope

But in a statement carefully balanced between endorsement of the principle of tenure and the "problems and potential for abuse in its execution," Chancellor Boyer also suggested that a tightening of the process by which tenure is granted on state campuses was also in order.

"The process by which tenure decisions are made," Dr. Boyer wrote, "must be strengthened to assure that continuing appointment in the university is extended only to those who have demonstrated the highest competence and whose future performance can be reasonably expected to be professionally excellent."

These views, amounting to a call for more stringent evaluation of faculty members up for tenure, are being echoed by college and university administrators across the country.

Public and private institutions alike are faced with the fact that enrollments have not kept pace with the rate at which faculty members were awarded life-long appointments.

This has raised the prospect that faculties may become "tenured in" with no room for new appointments, or that college departments may be forced to retain tenured teachers even though there are fewer students taking their courses than at the time they were granted tenure.

A spokesman for Dr. Boyer said yesterday that the lowering of the retirement age from 70 to 65, and the implementation of programs to reassign teachers from underenrolled courses could be accomplished by an order from the university system's board of trustees.

The Chancellor's policy statement was sent only to the 29 State University campuses that are entirely controlled by his office. Two state-related components of Cornell University and Alfred University, as well as the state's 38 locally sponsored community colleges, share their governance with other bodies.

Dr. Boyer said that his letter was in response to the re-evaluation of the existing tenure system as called for the university's 1972 master plan and to "the tenure debate which has intensified both within and outside the profession." He said his recommendations had been a result of consultations within the S.U.N.Y. community over the last six months.

An accompanying statement from the Chancellor's office said that "after appropriate further consultation with faculty, administration and students,"

Dr. Boyer would present "specific proposals" for the amendment of related university policies.

The City University's controversial new tenure policy requires special justifications for the awarding of job security to members of departments whose faculty is already more than half tenured. This policy is up for review, following intense criticism from the City University faculty union.

Name _____ Date _____

Year _____ Major _____

Grade Point Average _____ Sex _____

After you read the *New York Times* article, please answer the following two questions:

1. Assume you are an advisor to Chancellor Boyer. State for him the main political issue discussed in the article. Make your answer as specific as possible.

2. What strategy would you suggest that Chancellor Ernest L. Boyer pursue in handling the situation? Assume that you are providing recommendations for Chancellor Boyer. Make your response as pointed as possible, and make sure you are clear in what actions you recommend.

PARIS AGAIN BALKS A EUROPE ACCORD

Opposes Common Market Proposal for Consultation With U.S. on Policy

Special to The New York Times

LUXEMBOURG, April 2—Objections by France today blocked the nine Common Market countries from agreeing on improved procedures of consultation with the United States.

After six hours of talks here last night and this morning, the foreign ministers of the Nine agreed to meet in West Germany on May 4 and 5 for further consideration of how the United States should be consulted on joint European foreign policy initiatives that affect American interests.

The Nixon Administration has complained that the Common Market's newly developed system of making foreign policy decisions in common leaves no way for the United States to make its views known during early stages.

While France agreed today with her Common Market partners that some sort of preliminary exchange of views with the United States would be useful, the disagreement on how to achieve this was, as described by one top diplomat, "fundamental."

The nine foreign ministers examined the specific case of the Common Market's offer on March 4 of talks to Arab countries on long-range economic cooperation. The decision, which drew American complaints of a lack of consultation, was a tentative one, with Britain not participating fully because a Government change was under way.

Because of the dispute here, preliminary West European contacts with the Arabs, already delayed by the British reservation on the matter, are expected to be postponed again. At the same time there seems little hope for progress on other aspects of Atlantic relations between the United States and the Common Market until the dispute among the Nine is settled.

France Favors Limitation

France, represented here by Foreign Minister Michel Jobert, suggested a highly restricted form of consultations with the United States. He said that contacts should be made only when the Nine agreed that a particular case warranted them. He also suggested that such talks be held on the ministerial level.

The position adopted by the eight other countries was that there should be flexible talks with the United States on a regular basis covering a broad range of policy-making. Such talks, it was said, could be held on numerous diplomatic levels, including that of the foreign ministers and of lower-ranking diplomats.

This position, which was contained in a proposal made last month by Foreign Minister Walter Scheel of West Germany, is believed to be close to the system Secretary of State Kissinger is seeking. The secretary held talks with both West German and British leaders on the problem last week in Bonn and London.

According to a top West European official, the main reason that the French refused to agree on the broad consultation formula was that they were not confident of the ability of their partners to maintain independent policies under United States pressure.

Both the United States and the Common Market seem agreed that any new system of consultations before foreign-policy decisives would simply be an exchange of views to let each side take account of what the other was thinking. They reportedly envisage no legal obligation to harmonize policy since this is considered unworkable.

But France is said to fear that in a free-ranging consultation system the

United States could employ wide powers of persuasion, and much of the French suspicion on this score appears directed at Britain's new Labor Government, which has taken a strongly pro-American attitude since taking office early in March.

Britain, represented by Foreign Secretary James Callaghan, found herself isolated during a Common Market meeting here yesterday at which she said she would seek to change some of her basic arrangements with the Community. But in the following debate on consultation with the United States she found herself in the majority.

During these talks, Mr. Callaghan said Britain was ready to end her reservations about the Nine's holding contracts with the Arabs, but on condition that the question of how to inform the United States was resolved.

Repercussions of yesterday's announcement by Britain of her desire to renegotiate continued today. Cornelius Berkouwer, president of the European Parliament, attacked what he called Mr. Callaghan's supreme ignorance of the rules of the Common Market in saying that Britain would not be bound by her entry treaty if she did not get what she wanted in the renegotiations.

In what is considered a major snub, Mr. Callaghan refused to meet Mr. Berkouwer today to discuss the renegotiation problem.

Name_____ Date_____

Year _____ Major_____

Grade Point Average _____ Sex _____

After you read the *New York Times* article, please answer the following two questions:

1. Assume you are an advisor to an American government official. State for him the main political issue discussed in the article. Make your answer as specific as possible.

2. What strategy would you suggest the American government pursue with respect to this situation? Assume that you are providing recommendations for the American government. Make your response as pointed as possible and make sure you are clear in what actions you recommend.

Section One
PRINCE:
The Immaculate
Concept

Being an introduction to some notions about where you can find political problems and what to do with them after you find them.

A General Approach to Solving Political Problems

1

The title of this book blatantly—untastefully, some might say—capitalizes on one of the most famous works in the field of politics, *The Prince* by Machiavelli. Although it is rightfully considered a classic, *The Prince* was written to endear the author to the autocratic political rulers of semicivilized principalities located in what is now Italy. In this connection, if no other, we claim ancestry with Machiavelli, for this book was written by two twentieth-century political scientists trying to endear themselves to anyone (autocrat or not) who have to solve political problems.

The notion that people other than leaders will have the need for political strategies to solve political problems may be unfamiliar. Because *The Prince* was addressed to rulers, the idea has gained currency that only elites are fit for political action. From time to time the masses have been able to reduce the scope of an elite's political control, but seldom have they expected that non-elites were important political actors in their own right. As a result, ordinary citizens usually feel that they are above, below, or otherwise exempt from politics in daily life.

We most vehemently reject this notion. In our view, *a political problem is one in which you must get some other people to act or stop acting in a certain way in order to achieve a goal important to you.* We will bet that political problems constantly surround you. Until you recognize that they exist and learn to solve them, you will strike out more than you score—whether you have your eye on a better job, a successful sales pitch, or a new living mate, not to mention the more

3

conventional political goals like getting your friends into office and getting people already in office to make the policies you want.

Simply stated, politics means either getting people to do something they don't want to do or stopping them from doing something they would like to do. A candidate for office must get people to vote for him or her rather than that attractive charmer with the racy TV ads; candidates must also get people to turn off "Tuesday Night at the Movies" and distribute pamphlets in their neighborhoods. A secretary of state must get congressmen, journalists, and other doubters to leave him alone; at the same time he has to try to get stubborn foreigners to cooperate with his country's foreign policies. But politics pervades more than these grandiose areas of human life. For example, college students can find politics in their dormitories, extra-curricular activities and even their classroom.

We think it is not only true but also important that the problems faced by the candidate, the college students, or the president all boil down to *political* problems. To succeed they must all get a large number of individuals, groups, and institutions to "behave properly"—which, as any good politician knows, is an euphemism for getting them to do what he wants them to do. For the ordinary citizen, the number of individuals and the size of the groups and institutions may be smaller. Nevertheless, the problem is still the same.

The truth of this assertion will be argued out in the rest of the book. Let us put a word in here about the importance of this idea. If all sorts of people agree that there is a political dimension to their daily problems, there is a prospect that they will use political tools to solve these problems. Best of all, if we can expand the notion of what politics is and how successful political strategists operate, more people can become powerful political actors rather than mere political objects. The utopian day may come when political manipulation is banished from the earth. But in the meantime we feel something valuable is accomplished if at least those who are being manipulated can see what is happening to them. If such knowledge adds a little power and autonomy to other people's lives, so much the better.

We cannot blame Machiavelli for making his reputation by helping the elite. In his day, the only big spenders (and virtually the only literates) were the autocratic rulers. So the audience for his advice was rather narrow.

The Prince suggested using various combinations of the carrot (flattery and bribery) and the stick (assassination and forced retirement) to accomplish political goals. Obviously these techniques cannot be applied to daily politics. In any event, Machiavelli's genius was not prescribing how to act in particular situations, but rather providing a generalized view of the political world that leaders could use and apply to a wide variety of specific situations. Down through the years political leaders have taken ideas from Machiavelli, from other writers, and from their own experiences to formulate and update a working model, or political "game plan."

We think it is time to share some of the secrets of this game plan so they can serve as a guide to every man (and every woman, we hasten to add). No one's home is really a castle unless he knows how to act the way Machiavelli counseled his prince—that is, how to cope with the political problems of people, groups, and institutions encountered in daily life. We are going to present a plan for solving day-to-day political problems. Naturally, we cannot address the details of every possible specific problem. But we can do something more useful than provide advice on specific problems. We can, in the tradition of our adopted intellectual godfather, offer a tableau of guiding principles that can be applied to political problems as they come up. It is as if we were helping a traveler lost in a foreign city whose language he cannot read. We cannot tell him exactly where to go, but we can tell him how to translate the street signs. (We will, by the way, show how the general principles can be applied to a series of real and hypothetical political situations.)

Another of our hopes for those who use the system is that they will be able to experience the joy of participating in politics. The goals of politics, from the personal level on up, are often very serious and important. But the struggle to achieve those goals can be exhilarating. We hope that an understanding of our system will enlarge the number of participants who can appreciate this exhilaration and also increase the number of informed spectators who can vicariously participate in the fun of politics. To communicate this sense of joy we have taken a poetic liberty here and there in our descriptions of both hypothetical and real-world heroes. We mean no disrespect to any of them. Nor do we intend to demean the seriousness or relevance of our system by the medium in which we present it. That is a task we will leave to others.

The PRINCE
Political
Accounting System

2

To be successful in the politics of life, you must:

1. *Probe* your surroundings to figure who are the most important actors.
2. *Interact* with them to find out their inclinations and influence on the topics important to you.
3. *Calculate* how to get them to behave the way you want.
4. *Execute* your plans.

PRobe, INteract, Calculate, Execute: These are the moves we want to talk about in the following section. These words, by a happy coincidence, form the acronym PRINCE, and they nicely summarize the PRINCE system for solving political problems.

Our suggestions are based on the belief that one of the biggest obstacles to solving political problems is the limited capacity of the human mind to assemble, organize, and manipulate a large number of facts. After all, the fundamental rule for winning in the game of politics is well known to most politicians. It can be summed up quite simply: *Get more of the influential people, groups, and institutions on your side than against you.* The rule has obvious veracity when it comes to elections; it has equal truth for affecting the behavior of governmental officials or any other individual or group no matter what type of autocratic position they occupy. It also applies to high school principals, janitors, and gym teachers.

If the rule is so obviously true, why are there so many instances of political failure and political incompetences? One big reason is the in-

7

ability of people to acquire and use the information that would enable them to employ the rule. The successful political problem-solver has to acquire, remember, and utilize the names, positions of people, and their influence so that he can formulate a strategy to get the right people on his side at the right time. That this is the critical factor in determining political success is evidenced by looking at successful politicians. They usually have tremendous memories for detail. Equally strong evidence can be found by looking at the political blunders that are classics in history. They are usually explained by someone's forgetting to touch base with a certain individual or grease a certain path (or palm).

But even the most gifted political leaders cannot keep track of everything. They must pick out the few things that are most important for helping them succeed in whatever they want to do. Even so, the job would still be impossible if they had to figure out a new set of political factors every time they started working for a new goal. Just think what a mess a business would be in if it had to figure out a new way to judge its success or failure every year. To make their job simpler, businesspeople work with an agreed idea of assets and liabilities, profits and losses. Just so politicians. Their jobs are immensely more difficult because they have to work on an accounting system that will tell them how things *will* operate, rather than, like the business accountant, how things *have* operated. But this only means that the use of a clear and systematic method for assessing the balance of political forces is all the more important. Without such a scheme politicians could not have survived for all these years.

This book presents a scheme for recording the information necessary for you to solve whatever political problem faces you. That is what the PRINCE accounting system is all about. Once we have outlined the scheme and shown how others have used it, we will show how it can be used to line up on your side a preponderance of the influential people, groups, and institutions connected with a political problem important to you. Unfortunately, political problems are usually pretty complex. That is why the PRINCE political accounting system is fairly complicated. But before you reject it, remember that to win in politics you must do a lot of tedious things and pay careful attention to the facts of your situation. Bear with us, then, as we train you in the use of the PRINCE accounting system.

The first thing that we have to do is come up with a problem or two. That should not be too hard; most of us have our fair share. But it may not be too easy, either. Just any problem will not do. PRINCE will not cure your aching back, increase your reading speed, or improve your bowling score. (Although we shall see in a minute how it might help improve some people's chances of going bowling.) Two things have to be

#1

true about a problem before the PRINCE system can help you with it: (1) It has to be defined in terms of a relatively concrete outcome and (2) it has to be an outcome that can be brought about if some people who are now effectively blocking it can be made to change their position. The first point refers to the fact that *you have to know what you want—and be able to tell when you have got it*. It is no use stating a goal: "I want my congressman to represent me better." You have got to specify what bills you want him to support or oppose, what favors you want him to perform, or other specific actions. The second point is merely a restatement of our definition of politics, which is *getting people to change their behavior* so you can accomplish what you want.

#2

The next thing to be done is to develop a list of the people, groups, and institutions that stand in the way of achieving your goals. For purposes of brevity, let's call these people, groups, and institutions "political actors." The political accounting system will be only as good as the list of political actors you develop. Omitting any important person, group, or institution will doom your enterprise to failure. The size and nature of the list will vary from problem to problem. If your goal is to win the presidency of the United States, you might be tempted to list several hundred thousand people, but if you are trying to get a teacher to stop beating your eight-year-old, you might only have to deal with six or eight political actors. The basic rule is to include the people and groups who can most directly affect the disposition of the issues you are concerned with.

In dealing with large groups of political actors, it is obviously necessary to simplify. You do this by grouping the political actors into classes. This is why sensible presidential candidates divide the unmanageable number of potential voters into a manageable number of classes (blacks, whites, Republicans, etc.). Until the day comes when we all have a computer terminal in our homes, you will probably want to keep your list of political actors under ten. In most cases you will have no problem staying within this figure.

After you define the issues and actors you are going to subject to the PRINCE accounting system, the fun begins. The obvious critical thing about politics is deciding just who is important and why in effecting political outcomes—and, of course, also deciding how to change any predicted political outcomes you do not like.

To show how the system relates actors to one another, we will start with a concrete example of a family situation*—a lively, if often over-

*The family study presented in the first edition of this book was completed in the early 1960s. In this revised edition of *Everyman's PRINCE*, previous readers will note a reversal of issues important to the father and mother. The current family study reflects the role flexibility and reversals of the modern family, i.e., the mother demanding her right for a night out with her friends and the father becoming more clothes conscious.

looked, arena of political competition. Suppose that we are concerned with collective decisions within a five-member family consisting of mother, father, sister, brother, and the fifth member who is the mother's mother, the father's mother-in-law, and grandma to everyone else. Obviously, these would be the five political actors for this particular problem. We will assume that other potential family actors are not involved for one reason or another—they may not be on speaking terms, for example. For simplicity, let us assume that there are only five issues with which the five members of this family are concerned. (As with the list of political actors, the list of issues should be kept small.) These five issues are

1. Mother's right to bowl on Thursday nights
2. Father's right to unlimited clothing expenditures
3. Sister's desire to have her allowance increased from 10 to 15 cents (she is twelve years old)
4. Brother's freedom to stay out on weekday nights (he is ten)
5. A family visit to grandma's next week

(*Note that each issue is stated as a relatively specific decision that either will or will not be made.*)

#3

The first step in the system is to make our best estimate of how clearly each of the actors is for or against each of the issues. It usually happens in politics that some actors are decisively *for* a certain decision, others are just as decisively *against*, and still others are without a clear-cut opinion one way or the other. It might be possible to make a little notation of what each person wanted to happen on each issue: "definitely wants it to happen," "moderately opposed," "no opinion," etc. But recording positions this way wastes both paper and time. In these days of ecological sensitivity it is unfortunate to waste paper (which is, after all, recyclable), and a crime to waste time (which is not). Therefore, we suggest using numbers to record each actor's position on each issue. (The wary reader will rightly suspect that we have more devious reasons for using numbers; these will be unveiled in due time.) This can be done simply enough by using a positive number to indicate a favorable disposition to an issue and a negative number to indicate an unfavorable outlook. It helps to keep the numbers from ranging too widely, so assign a +3 to any actor who is clearly and unequivocally in favor of an issue and –3 to anyone clearly opposed.* Assign moderate positive or negative numbers to those who are moderately favorable or opposed.

*In the first edition of this book *issue position*, described above, and other variables were scaled to range from 0 to 10. In this edition we have scaled all variables between 0 and 3. This still permits a reasonably diverse summary of political situations, while at the same time allowing for easier procedures to estimate the different values.

For those whose opinion you do not know, as well as those who are known to have a neutral opinion, assign a zero. An example of such assignments is in Chart 2-1, which records the positions of each family member on each of the issues that concern him or her, with the list of actors down the side and the list of issues across the top. Note, for example, that the father is definitely in favor of unlimited spending, just as definitely opposed to mother's bowling, moderately opposed to sister's increased allowance, barely opposed to brother's night-time freedom, and dead set against visiting dear old grandma.

We had no trouble assigning these numbers because we made up the issues and the actors in this example. In analyzing actual situations, the first job is to find out who is for and against the issues you are concerned with and how strongly they are for and against. Sometimes you can find this out by talking to people; other times people make it quite clear how they feel by what they write, speeches they make, or in other ways. Other times it is necessary to make educated guesses on the basis of what you know about someone's general feelings, how someone has felt about previous issues, or whatever other clues you can find out about. Of course, there may be times when you simply cannot find out or reasonably guess someone's position on an issue; then you assign a zero. An issue is included only if at least one of your actors cares about it. In this example of family members (who are, quite typically, very much involved in one another's business) the only case of no opinion is brother's reaction about his sister's allowance. Chapter 10 contains a longer discussion of how to get data for a PRINCE analysis.

By itself this chart will predict what is most likely to happen *if the preference of each of the actors remained the same* and *if there were no other influences.* (We draw special attention to these qualifications because they are rather severely limiting conditions. We shall see how to get around them in a few minutes.) The answer can be simply derived

CHART 2-1. Political actors' issue positions.

| Political actors | Issues | | | | |
	Father spends	Mother bowls	Sister's allowance	Brother's freedom	Visit grandma
Father	+3	-3	-2	-1	-3
Mother	-2	+3	-1	-3	+3
Sister	+1	+1	+3	-1	+3
Brother	+2	-1	0	+3	-2
Grandma	-3	+3	+3	-3	+3
Total	+1	+3	+3	-5	+4

by adding up the columns. The highest positive number indicates the issue most likely to be resolved; the one with the highest negative number indicates the issue least likely to occur. If you add the columns in Chart 2-1, you see that "father spends" gets a +1, "mother bowls" gets a +3, "sister's allowance" gets a +3, "brother's freedom" gets a –5, and "visit grandma" gets a +4.

By looking at the numbers you can also see the tremendous importance of the grandma. Her positions are extreme so she cancels out what father and brother want and adds to the weight of what sister and mother want. What a difference in this political environment if she were isolated from the rest of the family! Fortunately for father and brother, however, it is necessary to take into account other factors than merely the simple issue positions of the political actors. We also have to consider the power of the actors on all of these issues, that is, the ability of each actor either to accomplish or prevent the occurrence of each outcome at issue.

Assigning power scores is much like assigning numbers to summarize the issue positions. It is probably easiest to start with those cases in which, if an actor really wants, he can, all by himself, either make the issue happen or prevent it from happening. In our family situation mother can, if she wishes, either go bowling or stay home. (Thinking about the personal problems she may encounter by going bowling may lead her to change her mind; but as far as power is concerned, once she has made up her mind, that settles the question.) Likewise, grandma has absolute power on the issue of a visit to her. She can feign illness and compel a family visit, or say she is not going to be home and so prevent the family from coming. Because we wish to keep the numbers in a reasonable range for the power accounting (just as we did on issue positions), we assign a 3 to actors on the issues where they have the resources for exercising complete control. We assign smaller numbers to actors on issues where they have less complete control (see Chart 2-2).

CHART 2-2. Power of actors on issues.

Political actors	Issues				
	Father spends	Mother bowls	Sister's allowance	Brother's freedom	Visit grandma
Father	3	2	3	3	1
Mother	1	3	2	2	3
Sister	1	1	1	1	1
Brother	1	1	1	2	1
Grandma	1	2	1	1	3

Note that the PRINCE accounting system does not allow for negative power. An actor either has or does not have power. All the numbers in the chart on power are positive. It would be possible to assign an actor a zero on an issue if he or she had absolutely no power. (But something to keep in mind when doing your own PRINCE analysis is that if you are assigning a lot of zeros in the power chart, you may not have the right combination of issues and actors.)

(It often happens that people are better placed to prevent something than they are to get it done, or vice versa. There are three ways to handle this problem) If they have a clearcut issue position, assign them a score on the basis of the power they have to do what they are most likely to do. For example, grandma might have much less blocking power on the issue of visiting her if she lived near the family so they always knew when she was home. We would still assign a 3 because her position is *not* in favor of preventing that decision, but is intended to make it happen. Another way to handle the problem is to give an average of the two power weights. This is probably the best choice if the power scores are not too far apart (say a difference of one or two points). If you are not certain enough of the actor's issue position to use the first solution and if the two power scores are so far apart that you do not want to use the second method, then just enter the actor's blocking power score. It is a pretty reliable rule of politics that the kind of power that counts most is the power to prevent things from happening. Therefore, if you are uncertain, that is the kind to include.

The numbers in Chart 2-2 can be used in connection with the numbers in Chart 2-1 to get a better prediction of what is likely to happen for each of these issues. This can be done by multiplying the appropriate numbers in the two charts. We have done that in Chart 2-3 by placing the numbers from Chart 2-2 in parentheses next to the numbers in Chart 2-1. Looking at the totals, we can see the effect of combining the

How to score an actor's power

CHART 2-3. Multiplying issue position times power.

Political actors	Issues				
	Father spends	Mother bowls	Sister's allowance	Brother's freedom	Visit grandma
Father	+3(3) = +9	−3(2) = −6	−2(3) = −6	−1(3) = −3	−3(1) = −3
Mother	−2(1) = −2	+3(3) = +9	−1(2) = −2	−3(2) = −6	+3(3) = +9
Sister	+1(1) = +1	+1(1) = +1	+3(1) = +3	−1(1) = −1	+3(1) = +3
Brother	+2(1) = +2	−1(1) = −1	0(1) = 0	+3(2) = +6	−2(1) = −2
Grandma	−3(1) = −3	+3(2) = +6	+3(1) = +3	−3(1) = −3	+3(3) = +9
Total	+7	+9	−2	−7	+16

power ratings with the issue position for each political actor on each issue. Now the visit to grandma and mother's bowling are the most likely, with sister's allowance moving from first to fourth.

Multiplying the two charts together gives us a different and somewhat more realistic picture of what is likely to happen. However, the PRINCE accounting system requires including another factor before we can have sufficient confidence in this particular aspect of the scheme. That factor we call *salience*—the *importance* each political actor attaches to the particular issue.

Salience is a little bit like issue position because it is based on what someone feels about an issue. And there may be quite a few cases where people will have strong opinions (close to +3 or –3 issue position) and will also have high salience. But salience is different from issue position. The cases where issue positions are strong while salience is low are very important to take note of in calculating political action. For example, some powerful political actors might be willing to accept an event that is contrary to their wishes because they do not care very much about that event. Hence, father might not care very much about sister's allowance because it involves such a relatively small amount of money. Father's lack of salience for this issue, then, might counteract the relatively high power he has over its outcome. Another time when it's important to look at salience is when an actor has an issue position close to zero. If he also has low salience, then you are safe in concluding that unless the situation changes he is not very important on that issue, no matter how high his power, because his zero issue position combined with low salience means he simply does not care one way or the other what happens. However, if he has zero issue position but very high salience, then you had better watch out. This means he cares a lot about the issue but has not yet been able to make up his mind. If and when he does decide, he is likely to be very active, and therefore important. We use the same format to record salience as we did with power. Assign a 3 to those who are most highly interested in the issue, and a zero to anyone who could not care less about it. (As with power, we do not allow for negative salience.) The scores for our little family are listed in Chart 2–4.

If you are getting into the swing of the political accounting system, you should have already guessed that we now must multiply the numbers in Chart 2–4 by the appropriate numbers in Charts 2–1 and 2–2. The result will be Chart 2–5, in which the first number in each cell is the issue position, the second number the power for the actor on that issue, and the third number the salience for the actor on the issue.

By now you might also guess some of the reasons we advocated recording information with numbers rather than words. Even with the

CHART 2-4. Salience of actors on issues.

| Political actors | Issues | | | | |
	Father spends	Mother bowls	Sister's allowance	Brother's freedom	Visit grandma
Father	3	3	1	3	1
Mother	1	3	2	2	3
Sister	1	1	3	1	2
Brother	1	2	1	3	1
Grandma	3	1	1	3	3

new math it is much easier to add and multiply numbers than words. You might notice two things that happen when you multiply the two charts together. The sign of an actor's issue position (that is, whether it is positive or negative) gives the positive or negative sign to the total score for the actor on the issue. His or her issue position puts the actor's power and salience either for or against the predicted outcome of the issue. The second thing is that if actors have a zero score on issue position, power, or salience, their whole score on that issue is wiped out. If you consider what a zero score on any of the three means, we think you will agree that this is a reasonable thing to happen. Look- ing at the totals, we can see the effect of including salience with power and issue position. The visit to grandma now looks like a certainty with father's spending moved from third back up to second as the most likely thing to happen. Brother's right to prowl becomes least likely.

Taken together, Charts 2-1 through 2-5 summarize the main ele- ments of the PRINCE political accounting system. Contained within those charts is a wealth of information about the political actors. This information can be used to figure out what is most likely to happen

CHART 2-5. Multiplying issue positions, power, and salience.

| Political actors | Issue | | | | |
	Father spends	Mother bowls	Sister's allowance	Brother's freedom	Visit grandma
Father	+3(3)(3) = +27	−3(2)(3) = −18	−2(3)(1) = −6	−1(3)(3) = −9	−3(1)(1) = −3
Mother	−2(1)(1) = −2	+3(3)(3) = +27	−1(2)(2) = −4	−3(2)(2) = −12	+3(3)(3) = +27
Sister	+1(1)(1) = +1	+1(1)(1) = +1	+3(1)(3) = +9	−1(1)(1) = −1	+3(1)(2) = +6
Brother	+2(1)(1) = +2	−1(1)(2) = −2	0(1)(1) = 0	+3(2)(3) = +18	−2(1)(1) = −2
Grandma	−3(1)(3) = −9	+3(2)(1) = +6	+3(1)(1) = +3	−3(1)(3) = −9	+3(3)(3) = +27
Total	+19	+14	+2	−13	+55

Gives us the likely outcome.

Doesn't tell us how to get to our way — unless of course we want to visit grandma.

Static.

Numbers:
Issue Position +3 → −3
Power +3 → 0
Salience +3 → 0

with a set of issues. What these charts taken together tell us is that three things—issue position, power, and salience—can be used to determine the likely outcome of the political process. However, as they stand, these charts do not provide us with much help in getting our way unless, of course, the existing distribution of issue position, power, and salience appears to point to what we want to happen. In other words, the scheme as presented so far is static. For it to be a useful guide to politics, we must make it dynamic.

To make our analysis dynamic, it is necessary to ask a question: "Under what conditions will issue position, power, and salience change?" Unfortunately, there are hundreds of such conditions, and they operate somewhat differently on each and every actor. Throughout the book we will describe some of these conditions. For the present, it is necessary to focus on one type of condition that is particularly important in the changing of issue position. This condition is concerned with the growth and decay of what are usually called *alliances* or *coalitions*.

Political actors will frequently "make deals" or support each other out of what might be called political friendship. If there is a strong history of a friendship bond between two actors, an alliance or coalition is likely to exist. The meaning of an alliance or coalition under this condition is that if two actors already agree on a series of issues, they are likely to agree when a new issue is presented to them. The important question to ask with respect to the dynamics of alliances and coalitions among political actors is the degree to which their friendship will lead one actor to agree with another out of political friendship.

The reverse is also true. Sometimes political actors have a strong history of disagreement on political issues. In this case they will likely oppose one another when facing a new issue. It is therefore important to determine the extent to which hostility will lead one actor to disagree with another for any given issue.

The final component of the PRINCE political accounting system is a chart that summarizes the friendship, neutrality, or hostility between any two actors. A sample chart based on the relationships of our hypothetical family (Chart 2-6) is presented below. A + is used to denote political friendship, a zero to denote political neutrality, and a – to denote political hostility. The three signs can be interpreted as a prediction of whether or not the actor in the row will attempt to agree with, remain neutral toward, or disagree with the actor designated by the column on any given issue the two are likely to become concerned with. It can be read, to take one pair of examples from it, that father (with a plus in sister's column) is likely to agree with sister's issue positions but that sister (with a minus in father's column) is not likely to agree with the father's issue positions.

CHART 2–6. Friendship-neutrality-hostility chart.

	Father	Mother	Sister	Brother	Grandma
Father	X	+	+	+	–
Mother	+	X	+	+	0
Sister	–	–	X	–	+
Brother	+	+	–	X	+
Grandma	–	+	+	+	X

The friendship-neutrality-hostility chart can help you predict which actors are more likely to agree or disagree with each other over the long haul by looking down the column of that actor. For example, looking down father's column, we would expect that the father could get mother or brother to back him easier than sister or grandma. These patterns are relatively stable and therefore can be used to gauge the degree to which changes in issue position might occur.

Let us briefly review what we have said about the PRINCE system so far. We suggest that you approach any situation that requires getting a collective decision as a political problem. You should undertake to attack this political problem by identifying the essential people, groups, or institutions—to use our jargon, political actors—who are important to your success and failure in solving your political problem. This list should be supplemented by a list of issues in which the political actors are involved. From these two lists you should construct four charts:

1. *Issue position* of political actors
2. *Power* of political actors on issues
3. *Salience* on the issues for the political actors
4. *Friendship-neutrality-hostility* patterns among the political actors

The information you gather is summarized below in Chart 2–7. Notice that issue position can have either positive numbers (if the actor in question favors a decision), negative numbers (if the actor opposes a decision), or zero (if the actor is neutral). Power and salience range from zero to 3—with no negative values. And friendship-neutrality-hostility is indicated by a plus, a zero, or a negative sign.

About the Rest of This Book

This chapter has painted a sketchy picture of the bare bones of the scheme that we advocate. It has given you the basic tool through which

CHART 2-7. Range of variables used in the PRINCE political accounting system and verbal interpretation of each variable.

Issue position	Power	Salience	Friendship-neutrality-hostility
+3 Strong support	+3 Strong power	+3 High salience	+ Tendency to agree with the actor in question
+2 Moderate support	+2 Moderate power	+2 Moderate salience	
+1 Weak support	+1 Weak power	+1 Low salience	
0 Neutrality	0 No power	0 No salience	0 Indifference toward the actor in question
−1 Weak opposition			
−2 Moderate opposition			− Tendency to disagree with the actor in question
−3 Strong opposition			

you can be as successful as Machiavelli's *Prince*. What remains now is to illustrate the tool for various types of political problems. In doing this, we will also present a more complete inventory of the way to use the information in the PRINCE charts. We hope to have these things happen: (1) you will come to understand the scheme better by seeing it applied to specific situations; (2) you will be given additional clues on how to use the scheme by looking at its utility for providing guidelines for political problem solving in different contexts; and (3) you might be seduced into thinking that the scheme is more valid if we warp some historical events and hypothetical cases to fit the structure of the PRINCE system. Each of the next seven chapters will apply the scheme to a particular political problem.

Section Two
The Ministry

Being a journey of the mind through real and imagined history to find instances of the use of the PRINCE system for solving political problems.

How the PRINCE System Produced the American Constitution

3

One of the mysteries of the American Constitutional Convention is why George Washington remained so passive during its sessions yet emerged from the convention as the first American political superstar. It can now be revealed that Washington was not passive at all, but was very actively, if quietly, applying a PRINCE analysis to what was happening. Many people then—and now—have thought that Washington was just another pretty face without any political skills to match his military successes. It has been argued that in politics he was just a front man for clever Machiavellian politicians. The truth of the matter is that he was himself a skillful politician employing the appropriate PRINCE charts at every occasion. Washington earned the title "father of his country," by first becoming every American's Prince.

In fewer than four months about forty men wrote a document that was a masterpiece and resolved the differences of a diverse collection of anti-British rebels who had only just begun to develop a conception of an American nation. Such a document was not produced before 1787, nor has one been produced since. At least one good explanation for what is universally ranked as one of the wonders of the political world is that someone was working the PRINCE accounting system. It seems clear to us that it had to be Washington, with his experience as a surveyor and his familiarity with using charts to get the lay of the land. While the rest of the guys were boozing it up in the Indian Queen, a local pub, on the evening of May 27, 1787, Washington was busy in his room with four empty PRINCE accounting system charts.

His first job was to reduce the forty-odd delegates to a manageable

21

number of political actors. His limit, as we indicated in the first chapter, was ten political actors.

He was helped in this task first by the rules of the convention that provided for voting by state delegations rather than individuals. He had to deal with only twelve actors—the thirteen former colonies minus Rhode Island, whose delegates boycotted the meeting. This was probably close enough to the ideal upper limit of ten, but because it was summer Washington looked for other ways to make his job easier by reducing the number of actors.

PRINCiple 3.1:* To simplify the PRINCE charts, lump together actors who have strong common interests.

For the sake of simplicity, George Washington lumped the actors together. Washington called South Carolina, North Carolina, and Georgia the *Deep South*. The Deep South states had similar economic interests that were different from those of the North, including most significantly a reliance upon slave labor. Therefore Washington expected, quite rightly, that they would act together on a wide range of issues. George called New Jersey, Delaware, Connecticut, New York, and Maryland the *States' Righters*. The States' Righters were small states worried about their continued influence in any new arrangements, plus New York, a majority of whose delegates also worried about states' rights because they wanted a weak central government. George treated Massachusetts and New Hampshire as one. These two states also had similar economic interests, plus a long background of cultural affinity and close cooperation between their citizens. There were only two states treated separately—Pennsylvania, the state of Ben Franklin, and George's own state, Virginia. Washington thus ended up with five actors: (1) the Deep South, (2) the States' Righters, (3) Massachusetts-New Hampshire, (4) Pennsylvania, and (5) Virginia.

After defining the actors, George got out his PRINCE charts and went to the next problem—identifying issues. The first issue was whether the convention would try to make the thirteen states into one nation or just strengthen their existing alliance against England. The convention had been organized for the official purpose of amending the old constitution, the Articles of Confederation. But Washington and some of the other leaders, like Benjamin Franklin, thought that the old constitution was such a mess that an entirely new one should be written.

---

*Look for these inserts throughout the case studies in each section. They summarize important points made by the case.

They also wanted a new constitution so that the thirteen states could be bound into one nation. Thus Issue 1 was whether the convention should write an entirely new constitution that would create a nation or amend the old constitution that would simply make the existing confederation stronger.

PRINCiple 3.2:   Identify issues in terms of relatively specific outcomes.

The second major issue was how strong the federal executive should be. A few delegates like Alexander Hamilton wanted a king, but most of the delegates had had their stomachs full of kings. So Issue 2 was whether they would have a strong executive by electing one person for a reasonable period of time (at least four years or more) or a weak executive by electing more than one person for a short period of time.

Related to this question was a third issue—how the executive (the president) was to be elected. Those who favored a strong executive wanted election by the people. Others, however, opposed this procedure and wanted the president elected by the states or, in a few cases, by the Congress. So Issue 3 was whether the president would be elected by the people.

Another set of issues had to do with the legislature. First was the question of *how* the states should be represented in Congress. The delegates from the larger states wanted congressional seats distributed according to the proportion of the population in each state. Of course the delegates from the small states weren't stupid; they knew that if representation was based on population they would always be outvoted. Therefore they opposed proportional representation and wanted each state to have the same number of seats. Washington saw that the question of proportional representation in the legislature would be Issue 4.

If the states were going to be represented by population, however, a question would arise whether slaves would be counted as people and thereby increase the population of the slave states. The question of counting slaves became Washington's Issue 5.

Two issues had to do with the powers of Congress, in particular whether Congress would have the power to (1) tax exports and (2) regulate the slave trade. The latter boiled down to whether Congress would abolish the slave trade. These two issues were 6 and 7 respectively. *tax exports* → *abolish slave trade*

Because many of the delegates had been forced to read Montesquieu when they were students, they became obsessed with the idea that a good government needed an executive, a legislature, and a judiciary.

Although there was a consensus that there should be a supreme court in the capital, not all agreed that there should be federal courts in the states. Hence, Issue 8 was whether the federal courts should operate within states.

Realizing that the delegates would probably spend most of the beautiful summer of 1787 cooped up indoors debating these eight substantive issues, George knew that they would still have two very important procedural issues left: (1) how the Constitution was to be amended and (2) how the Constitution was to be ratified. Having gotten wind of the scuttlebut from the delegates, Washington knew that amending the Constitution would be Issue 9—whether the delegates would accept a proposed amendment procedure that allowed the Constitution to be amended by three-fourths of the states or would favor some other plan such as unanimous consent by all the states, which would in effect give each state a veto.

Washington's final issue dealt with the ratification process. He defined Issue 10 as the ratification of the Constitution by the people rather than by the states through their legislatures.

Washington could have defined a number of other issues, but he felt that these gave him enough of an idea of the major disputes and results of the convention. He then made a list of the ten issues and a label for each issue that he would use on his PRINCE charts. The list was:

1. The purpose of the convention is to write a new constitution and thereby create a nation. Label: *Nation.*
2. A strong executive will be created. Label: *Exec.*
3. People shall elect the president. Label: *Presid.*
4. Representation in the legislature will be according to population. Label: *Legis.*
5. Slaves will be counted as part of a state's population. Label: *Slaves.*
6. Congress will have the power to tax exports. Label: *Exports.*
7. Congress will have the power to regulate, and hence to abolish, the slave trade. Label: *Slave Trade.*
8. Federal courts shall be established in the states. Label: *Courts.*
9. Only three-fourths of the states are needed to amend the Constitution. Label: *Amend.*
10. Ratification of the Constitution by the people. Label: *Ratif.*

Having identified the basic issues as well as the primary political actors, Washington now had the columns and rows of the four PRINCE

CHART 3-1. Political actors' issue positions.

Actors	Nation	Exec.	Presid.	Legis.	Slaves
			Issues		
Deep South					
(Ga., S.C., N.C.)	+3	+3	+2	+3	+3
States' Righters					
(N.Y., N.J., Del., Conn., Md.)	−3	−1	−3	−3	−2
Massachusetts-New Hampshire	+3	+3	+3	0	−3
Pennsylvania	+3	+3	+3	−3	−3
Virginia	+3	0	+3	+3	+3
	Exports	*Slave trade*	*Courts*	*Amend.*	*Ratif.*
Deep South					
(Ga., S.C., N.C.)	−3	−3	−3	−3	+3
States' Righters					
(N.Y., N.J., Del., Conn., Md.)	+2	+2	−2	−2	+1
Massachusetts-New Hampshire	0	+2	+3	+3	+3
Pennsylvania	+2	+2	+3	+2	+3
Virginia	−3	+2	+3	+2	+2

charts labeled. He then proceeded to estimate the numbers necessary to fill up the cells of the charts.

> PRINCiple 3.3: Use the PRINCE system to project the voting decisions of legislative bodies.

He started with the issue position—Chart 3-1. He scored a +3 when there was agreement among the members of the coalitions for a particular formulation and −3 when there was agreement against it. When there was not full agreement, he scored somewhere between 1 and 3, depending upon how strong a consensus was for or against the proposal among each coalition-actor.

Washington then moved on to Chart 3-2—the power of each actor for each issue. He gave each group a power of 1, except the States' Righters, whom he gave a power of 2. He thus employed an abbreviated form of Chart 3-2.

The information in Chart 3-3 proved critical for Washington and the American Constitutional Convention because it registered the salience of the issues for each of the actors. Chart 3-3 indicates the importance Washington thought each of the actors had for each of the issues. One can see how critical salience is by first multiplying Charts 3-1 and

CHART 3-2. Power of the actors on issues.

Actors	Power for all issues
Deep South (Ga., S.C., N.C.)	1
States' Righters (N.Y., N.J., Del., Conn., Md.)	2
Massachusetts-New Hampshire	1
Pennsylvania	1
Virginia	1

3-2 and comparing the product to Charts 3-1, 3-2, and 3-3 multiplied together. Chart 3-4 presents the sums of the columns, which is an indicator of what is likely to happen.

If salience were not figured into the PRINCE system, Washington would have been particularly despondent. Without salience, there seems to be only clearcut support for the ratification procedure and a strong executive. All the rest of the figures are borderline. However, the addition of salience indicates a strong commitment for creating a union, a strong executive, counting slaves as population, and the amendment and ratification procedures. There also appears to be a strong commitment against a legislature based on a proportion of the population and the power of Congress to tax exports.

> PRINCiple 3.4: Always remember to consider salience when making a compromise. It's frequently prudent to offer a little extra to the side with the higher salience.

Washington assumed that 20 points was a cutoff for consensus on an issue (+ for and – against) and concluded that a large number of compromises would be necessary to produce a strong constitution. Realizing the need for compromise, he formulated a strategy on his part that would keep any single political actor from pulling out of the convention. To help him do this, he completed Chart 3-5 of the PRINCE system.

Washington was particularly wary of *polarization*, a phenomenon that has rendered many meetings and some political systems hopelessly confused. Polarization is the degree to which the political actors are split into two opposing camps. The degree to which there are no actors in the system who are friendly with the enemies of other actors is an

CHART 3-3. Salience of actors on issues.

Actors	Issues				
	Nation	Exec.	Presid.	Legis.	Slaves
Deep South					
(Ga., S.C., N.C.)	3	2	1	2	3
States' Righters					
(N.Y., N.J., Del., Conn., Md.)	2	3	2	3	1
Massachusetts-New Hampshire	3	2	1	3	1
Pennsylvania	3	2	1	3	1
Virginia	3	3	1	3	3
	Exports	Slave trade	Courts	Amend.	Ratif.
Deep South					
(Ga., S.C., N.C.)	3	3	3	1	1
States' Righters					
(N.Y., N.J., Del., Conn., Md.)	3	1	2	1	1
Massachusetts-New Hampshire	3	1	2	3	1
Pennsylvania	2	1	3	3	1
Virginia	3	0	3	3	2

indication of polarization. In contrast, the degree to which friends and enemies are thoroughly mixed indicates a basically depolarized system.

> PRINCiple 3.5:   Polarization is destructive and consensus is constructive if you are on the side of the consensus. If you are not, the converse is true.

Washington employed a simple procedure for calculating the polarization level of the convention. He ranked all pairs of actors at the convention as friendly, neutral, or hostile. Chart 3-6 indicates how the political actors were ordered.

Washington breathed a sigh of relief when he examined the list. He discovered that the actors were relatively depolarized, because Virginia as well as Massachusetts-New Hampshire provided friendly links between most of the hostile pairs. The major threat of polarization came from the fact that the States' Righters group was hostile toward both Pennsylvania and Virginia and the Deep South was also hostile towards Pennsylvania. This situation created the possibility of two camps forming—one around Pennsylvania and Virginia and the other around the Deep South and States' Righters. Although the situation was relatively depolarized at the outset, conditions existed for hostility be-

CHART 3-4. Predicted issue outcomes with and without salience.

	Issues				
	Nation	Exec.	Presid.	Legis.	Slaves
Charts 3-1 × 3-2 (Without Salience)	+6	+7	+5	-3	-4
Charts 3-1 × 3-2 × 3-3 (With Salience)	+24	+12	+5	-12	+8
	Exports	Slave trade	Courts	Amend.	Ratif.
Charts 3-1 × 3-2 (Without Salience)	0	+7	+2	0	+13
Charts 3-1 × 3-2 × 3-3 (With Salience)	-2	-1	+7	+14	+15

CHART 3-5. Friendship-neutrality-hostility chart.

This actor	Feels about this actor:				
	Deep South	States' Righters	Massachusetts- New Hampshire	Penn- sylvania	Virginia
Deep South		-	-	-	+
States' Righters	-		+	-	-
Massachusetts- New Hampshire	-	+		+	-
Pennsylvania	-	-	+		+
Virginia	+	-	-	+	

tween the two potential camps to grow and for the convention to fail as a result of that growth.

Fortunately, Washington had a couple of things going for him. One of the most important was that he was a member of the prestigious Virginia delegation. Realizing that he was something of a national hero, he concluded that if he took public positions and got involved directly in the issues, he would generate a break between the camps. He concluded that his role was to be passive in public and at formal meetings but to work actively for compromise behind the scenes. He could also keep Virginia from antagonizing the States' Righters if he played a consensus-building role.

Washington also was fortunate to have Benjamin Franklin in the Pennsylvania delegation. By far, Benjamin was *the* star of the con-

CHART 3-6. Pairs of actors ordered from friendly to neutral to hostile.

Pair of actors	Friendship-neutrality-hostility score
Pennsylvania-Virginia	+
Pennsylvania-Massachusetts/New Hampshire	+
Deep South-Virginia	+
States' Righters-Massachusetts/New Hampshire	+
Deep South-Massachusetts/New Hampshire	−
Virginia-Massachusetts/New Hampshire	−
Deep South-States' Righters	−
Deep South-Pennsylvania	−
Pennsylvania-States' Righters	−
Virginia-States' Righters	−

vention which meant that Pennsylvania delegates would follow his lead and that delegations from other states would be open to his views. Washington got to him before the convention and convinced him (we are not sure whether he used the PRINCE system or just appealed to Franklin's enormous ego) to modify Pennsylvania's view and to seek compromise with the other states.

Another fortunate factor that operated to the advantage of those who wanted a successful convention was that the States' Righters and the Deep South had a moderate degree of antagonism toward each other. Washington's plan—to make sure that the two groups did not form a coalition against the rest of the actors—was greatly aided by the basic antagonism the two groups had for each other. It was not a sufficiently strong antagonism to prevent them from cooperating (as was, for example, the antagonism between Virginia and the States' Righters) but it was sufficient to prevent the two groups from joining together and wrecking the convention.

> PRINCiple 3.6: Compromise occurs on issues about which there is no consensus if actors have a consensus on other issues.

The charts helped Washington in many ways. For example, he could see that the strong executive (Issue 2) was uncertain of victory. The favorable actors—Deep South, Massachusetts-New Hampshire, and Pennsylvania—had only six votes (out of twelve). Washington's own state,

CHART 3-7. Score sheet comparing the PRINCE system to actual results.

	PRINCE analysis of events most likely to occur	
Issue	PRINCE total score	Actual results
1 *(Nation)*	+24	Occurred as stated
10 *(Ratif.)*	+15	Occurred as stated
9 *(Amend.)*	+14	Occurred as stated
2 *(Exec.)*	+12	Occurred as stated
5 *(Slaves)*	+8	Occurred but with slaves counting as three-fifths
8 *(Courts)*	+7	Compromise by leaving to Congress to decide
3 *(Presid.)*	+5	Compromise using electoral college instead of people
7 *(Slave Trade)*	−1	No regulating until 1808
6 *(Exports)*	−2	Rejected as stated
4 *(Legis.)*	−12	Most highly debated issue with a 50-50 compromise effected

Virginia, was so evenly divided that the delegation frequently was dead-locked and was unable to vote. (Note that Virginia has a zero issue position, but a saliency of 3 on this issue.) The idea was to get some of the States' Righters, who were only moderately opposed, to support a strong executive. As he looked at his friendship-neutrality-hostility chart he could see that it would be very unwise for anyone from Pennsylvania or the Deep South to lobby for a strong executive. The States' Righters had hostility toward both Pennsylvania and the Deep South. However, the Massachusetts-New Hampshire group was viewed more positively by the States' Righters, so Washington knew that they would be more likely to listen favorably to appeals from one of the New England delegation.

Washington also used his PRINCE calculations to plan where and how to make compromises that led to a successful consensus. On the question whether to count slaves as part of the population, it was clear that some compromise would have to be made. At first Washington thought of proposing to split the difference and count slaves as one-half, which is a common bargaining strategy. But he looked at the salience figures and saw that the proponents of counting slaves, the Deep South and Virginia, held their view with higher salience than the opponents who did not want to count slaves at all. So he suggested giving the South and Virginia slightly more than half and counting slaves as three-fifths of the population—bizarre from a humanistic viewpoint, but quite sound politically. On the other hand, when Washington looked at the salience for how legislative representation should be based (Issue 4) he saw that both sides held their views with equally high salience. Therefore he was attracted to the notion—which was finally accepted—of having two houses of the legislature, one to satisfy the views of each side.

It should also be clear that the decisions made by the convention rarely placed the States' Righters and the Deep South on the same side. A decision not to count slaves but to use proportional representation for determining representatives to the legislature would have done this. Instead, there was a compromise on both issues so that neither side would be alienated.

Another strategy followed by the convention was to avoid certain critical issues. Hence, the decision to end the importation of slaves was not to take effect until 1808—twenty-one years after the convention— and the question of the role of the federal courts was to be dealt with in the Congress itself.

Two of the time-worn patterns of compromise appeared to be most important here: One is to give each party half of the pie, which was implemented in the decisions on proportional representation and counting slaves, and the other is to postpone the consequence of the decision, if not the decision itself.

Patterns of Compromise

The PRINCE system gave Washington a picture of the areas of conflict and the actors most likely to disagree. As Table 3–7 shows, it forecast the convention results with notable accuracy. From this picture he was able to create an atmosphere of compromise by playing a quiet and unifying public role and a private role that worked for compromise. Fortunately for him and the new union, the predispositions of the actors were basically in the direction with which Washington agreed, which allowed him to play a consensus role in dealing with the convention. As we will see in the next chapter, it is sometimes necessary for those using the PRINCE system to play the role of breaking up existing agreements to get basic change. During the Constitutional Convention, Washington had only to insure an atmosphere of trust and compromise to achieve his purposes.

The Career of Ralph Nader: PRINCE vs. Big Business

4

When we speak of people in society, we casually say that people both shape and are shaped by their social environment. But the fact of the matter is that for those few people who fundamentally change their environment, there are thousands more who merely adapt to their surroundings. This is certainly true for those who are comfortably rewarded by things as they are; and it is no less true for those who at one time in their lives were prompted to bring about change. Some would-be reformers are defeated by the rigidity of the status quo; others soon see their energies dissipated in trying to attack all the pivotal points of a system at once; still others become tired from the struggle against long-enduring forces of the existing system. The endless roster of those who have challenged society and lost makes all the more intriguing the story of those few who have challenged and won.

Ralph Nader is one such person. Few people in recent American history have made such an impact upon social values, governmental policy, and American society in general at such a young age. (He was only thirty-two when he catapulted into fame.) His successes have depended on intelligence, hard work, integrity, and a reasonable amount of good luck. But more than this, a study of his career shows that Nader has put all these assets together with a political style that corresponds perfectly to the dictates of the PRINCE accounting system. Although a number of factors that cannot be attributed directly to his reliance on PRINCE have been crucial to Nader's successes, we can have little doubt after studying his decisions that Nader's skillful approach to reforming American society closely conforms to the guidelines of the PRINCE system.

It is also clear that by conforming to the PRINCE system he has been able to outdo countless idealistic would-be reformers.

Like many "overnight sensations," Nader's early career was marked by hard work, dedication, and a singular lack of success. While still in Harvard Law School, he actively expressed his disappointment with the inadequacies of American society. He focused his attention not on the government, but on big business as the locus of power creating substantial malfunction of the social system. In particular, he lamented the policies of the automotive industry in producing automobiles that contributed as much menace as good to the society that used them. This most significant expression of his views was in an article he published on automobile safety for the *Harvard Law Record*. After graduating he took a job with a law firm in Connecticut and continued to interest himself in automobile safety. During the period 1960–1964, he published several articles on the subject. He also involved himself in the movement to get the state legislatures in Connecticut and neighboring New York and Massachusetts to pass auto safety laws; these efforts came to nothing.

It seems reasonable to speculate that during this period Nader must have developed deep frustration at the ease with which the power-holders in government and industry permitted the continued production of automobiles that resulted in injury, destruction, and death for the American people. Many people confronted with such frustrations have rejected political solutions to their problems, either by turning off their concerns with social affairs altogether or else by escalating their hostility to the point of demanding revolutionary overthrow of the system—cries that seem to be self-satisfying to the demanders in direct ratio to how self-defeating they are for actually getting anything done.

It is also interesting to note that Nader did *not* decide to work through the electoral political process, a tactic frequently recommended for effectively working within the established system. He probably knew that such tactics as running for office on a single-issue platform, seeking out other candidates with the "right" issue position, or trying to establish a separate political party to advance his programs and goals has traditionally been one of the most certain ways to dissipate and destroy movements devoted to change. He knew that political campaigns were *almost never* decided on the basis of a single issue and that a single issue has *never* been the basis for long-run political success. He also knew that the American people have been conspicuously unattracted to candidates and parties that propose to carry out a detailed agenda of specific changes. He knew that the best he could hope for by working through the electoral process was to join a group that would be successful by carrying out the traditional favors, constituency services, and provision of general promises by which people get elected. Such a group might be able to pay some attention to the subject of his concern, auto safety, but such attention would be marginal at best.

> PRINCiple 4.1: Include actors relevant to your issue and issues relevant to those actors even if the issues are irrelevant to you.

Nader's successes were not to come from the ballot, but from the PRINCE political accounting charts. In setting up Chart 4-1, the issue positions of the relevant political actors, it is important to notice that although Nader chose not to become active on civil rights or the Vietnam war, it is nevertheless important to include them in the chart. The reason for this is important in planning any political strategy: It is necessary to include the actors who are relevant to the issues you care about—and then go on to include the issues that these actors care about. In dealing with the national political system, it would be possible to construct an almost endless list of issues and actors. But, remembering to keep the system as simple as possible, let's work with a chart with three issues and seven actors. The issues are *auto safety*, defined in Nader's terms as the manufacture of automobiles possessing specified safety characteristics; *civil rights*, defined as the elimination of formal and informal rules by which minority groups, primarily blacks, are denied basic rights that others enjoy; and *Vietnam*, defined as the continued military effort to achieve a stable pro-United States regime in South Vietnam.

From Nader's point of view there were seven identifiable actors who were important for his purposes. The first three were more-or-less well defined institutional actors: the *executive branch* officials who would be important in both initiating and ultimately administering any legis-

CHART 4-1. Issue positions of political actors.

	Auto safety	Civil rights	Vietnam
Executive	−1	+2	+3
Congress	+1	+1	+1
Industry	−3	+1	+1
Left wing	+3	+3	−3
Liberals	+2	+2	−3
Conservatives	−2	−1	+2
Right wing	−3	−3	+3

lation on auto safety; the *Congress*, which would have to pass any such legislation; and the representatives of the *auto industry*, who would, of course, clearly proclaim their views on the issue. The four remaining "actors" were in fact segments of the mass public, divided into groups likely to manifest identical responses to the issues: the small *left wing*, a larger moderate left or *liberal* segment of the public, a segment of the moderate right or *conservative* element of the public about the same size as the liberals, and a small group of extreme conservatives or the *right wing*.

Looking at Chart 4-1, which relates the actors to the issues, we can presume that Nader's preferences were fairly close to those reported for the left wing. He might well have felt that the "natural" thing for him to do would be to pursue all his ideals simultaneously and therefore to associate himself with one or more versions of left-wing politics. But we have already noted that Nader was more interested in achieving results than in merely consorting with like-minded ideologues. So he decided not to submerge himself in the left wing (which would certainly have prevented his becoming an important force for change).

> PRINCiple 4.2: Ideology should be a political tool, not
>   a philosophical crutch. Don't let ideology deter-
>   mine all your issue positions.

But even this decision, insightful though it was, did not end his problems of political strategy. A major obstacle that still remained was that the goal he had chosen to seek—auto safety—was given lipservice support by everyone who talked about the subject. Government, industry, and others who discussed the topic all agreed that auto safety, like patriotism, was a good thing. The trouble was that like patriotism, which governments invoke to secure support for their policies, auto safety was a symbol frequently invoked not to produce any change in society but rather to buttress the status quo. In particular, the auto industry had successfully sold a definition of auto safety that blamed accident injuries not on automobile design but on drivers' errors and incompetence. Much to the satisfaction of the auto industry, the consensus was that the most dangerous part of the automobile was the "nut behind the wheel." This consensus was so widespread among the industry and the public that when the Ford Motor Company did try to offer some minor safety features in the 1950s, such as padded dashboards, they were made optional extras, just like white-wall tires or cigarette lighters. And the consumers, constantly being told by the industry, the National Safety Council, and others that the driver was the main cause of death and injury, refused to pay extra money for mechanical safety features.

So Nader was faced with the formidable task of redefining the issue so that it would point to some action other than the endless—and fruitless—public campaigns for "driver safety." He chose to do this by doing some very tedious research not only on what made accidents happen, but also on *what happened in accidents*. Nader's orientation was not toward the impossible task of turning America's 80 million drivers into teetotalling "little old ladies from Pasadena," which was in effect what had been tried before. Instead, he concentrated on showing how design and construction of automobiles made accidents more likely and—more important—how design and construction turned even the most minor collisions into destructive, lethal tragedies.

As a result of his research, which he published in *Unsafe At Any Speed*, Nader was able to come up with a definition of auto safety that allowed him to draw the line between his supporters and his opponents. His extensive research enabled Nader to show conclusively that not reckless drivers but unsafe cars were the primary cause of death, injury, and damage in accidents. The solution to the problem then was to pass laws that controlled the manufacturer as well as the driver. Nader wanted the government to create safety standards that all new cars must meet to be legally sold. His research allowed him to recommend standards that were very specific, described in highly technical language, and in many cases scientifically tested. He recommended seat belts (both lap and shoulder); bolted front seats; a collapsible steering wheel; failsafe brakes; safety tires; padded recessed dashboards; shock absorbent, nondamageable bumpers; the elimination of sharp edges in the exterior design; and numerous other mechanical changes.

With the publication of his provocative, carefully researched book, Nader began not only to redefine the issue so that something could be done about it, but also to begin to gain power over the outcome. His book established his expertise on the subject—and an expert reputation is a growing source of political power in our complex technological society. In Nader's case, at least, it was to be a source of much more power than wealth, personal charm, violence, or other resources that people commonly try to exploit to secure power.

> PRINCiple 4.3: In an increasingly complicated society, knowledge is important to establish an actor's power on an issue.

The redefinition of the issue also helped clarify the political task confronting him. He could see that his problem was to change the system with which he had to work. It was a more difficult task than, for example, that which confronted George Washington in the Constitutional Convention, where he merely had to capitalize on existing positions and salience concerning the issues. Unlike Washington, who essentially had to cover up animosities among political actors, Nader was forced to emphasize them.

To get a more complete picture of the task confronting Nader, let us look at the PRINCE political accounting charts for salience and power. These charts indicate that the situation in 1965 was heavily stacked against Nader. The net interaction of issue position, salience, and power (found, as you recall, by multiplying Charts 4-1, 4-2, and 4-3 together) produced the following results for each actor on the auto safety issue:

	Auto safety
Executive	-2
Congress	+2
Industry	-27
Left wing	+3
Liberals	+2
Conservatives	-4
Right wing	-3
Total	-29

This accounting shows a massive political deficit on the issue, even though there was not a great deal of opposition outside the industry. But the high salience and power of the industry, plus a low amount of opposition by the executive and right wing public opinion resulted in the substantial negative balance that existed in the mid-sixties. An analysis of the components of the industry score indicates the crucial factor of business's capacity to regulate itself. This allows it 3 power

CHART 4-2. Salience on issues for political actors.

	Auto safety	*Civil rights*	*Vietnam*
Executive	1	2	3
Congress	1	2	3
Industry	3	1	1
Left wing	1	2	3
Liberals	1	2	3
Conservatives	1	2	2
Right wing	1	3	3

CHART 4-3. Power on issues for political actors.

	Auto Safety	Civil rights	Vietnam
Executive	2	2	3
Congress	2	1	1
Industry	3	1	1
Left wing	1	1	1
Liberals	1	1	1
Conservatives	2	2	2
Right wing	1	3	1

units, which jacks up its score for those issues on which it has a strong position and a high salience.

Chart 4-2, which reports on salience, shows that there was almost no interest for the issue within the executive, Congress, and among the public. These charts show that getting the right people interested was at least as important as getting people to change their minds.

Politics, we are often told, is the art of the possible. Even a dedicated idealist like Nader had to pick and choose as to which actors he could get to agree with his position. Chart 4-4, which shows the relative friendship, neutrality, and hostility among the actors, provides some important clues as to where to pick and choose. In particular, it emphasizes the danger of closely aligning with the left wing in his political strategy. Even though they were highly receptive to his views, their active support would do little to help bring about the desired changes by anyone else. (The same may be said for the right wing, of course. But it was scarcely a serious question whether he should try to get their support, any more than that of the auto industry, whose financial interests dictated a rigid opposition in the political context of that time.) He was left with trying to convince the executive and factions of the public to adopt a more favorable position on the auto safety issue.

> PRINCiple 4.4: Ignore actors who want to be your political friends if those actors don't have any other friends or don't have power.

In planning political action, the point is inevitably reached where it is necessary either to ignore or to suffer the opposition of some actor concerned with an issue, even though it would be highly desirable to have his or her power on your side. There are many reasons for this. It may be that an actor is so strongly against your position that it would be im-

CHART 4–4. Friendship-neutrality-hostility chart.

This actor	Feels about this actor						
	Execu- tive	Con- gress	Indus- try	Left wing	Liberals	Conserva- tives	Right wing
Executive	X	+	+	–	+	–	–
Congress	–	X	+	–	+	+	–
Industry	+	+	X	–	0	+	+
Left wing	–	–	–	X	–	–	–
Liberals	+	+	–	+	X	–	–
Conservatives	0	+	+	–	–	X	+
Right wing	–	–	+	–	–	+	X

possible, or at least too costly in terms of resources and time, to bring him or her around to your point of view. This is how Nader felt about industry and the right wing. It may be that adding an actor will so alienate your current supporters that the cohesion of your coalition is threatened. This is how Nader felt about the left wing.

The danger in making the necessary exclusionist choices is that those left out may get together and form a concern of sufficient issue position, salience, and power to defeat you. Fortunately, as the friendship-neutrality-hostility chart clearly indicates, Nader had little to fear from a counter-coalition in this case. The left wing was archenemy with both industry and the right wing. And industry, while its orientation was to the right of center on many issues, preferred a "respectable" posture that led it to disassociate itself as sharply from the extreme right wing as from the left wing.

However, the friendship-neutrality-hostility distribution was by no means ideal. On the one hand, members of the potential coalition—the executive, Congress, liberals, and conservatives—held only moderate attraction for one another, at best. On the other hand, there were some friendship bonds between each of the potential coalition members with at least one of the members of the excluded coalition, especially toward industry. The most important problem was how to keep industry from convincing would-be supporters not to favor the imposition of safety standards on the manufacture of automobiles.

One sure way to prevent industry from wooing supporters away from Nader would be to raise the salience of the auto safety issue, defined as it was to point out the faults of the industry. Such action would simultaneously increase the relative importance of the favorable issue positions that existed, help to neutralize the high salience felt by the industry, and also tend to lower the friendship that the potential allies of Nader felt toward the industry. They would therefore be more likely to change their positions away from that of the industry.

Contemplating this course of action undoubtedly put Nader in a quandary, because raising the salience of political issues in the arena of national politics is not an easy task. Public attention is an extremely scarce commodity.

As frequently happens to political actors, Nader had good reason to wonder if he would ever get his salience up. He had been writing about auto safety since the late fifties as a law student. He had tried in Massachusetts, Connecticut, and New York to get auto safety legislation passed at the state level. He had testified before these state legislatures, but to no avail. In 1964 he went to Washington, D.C., and did the same thing he had done on the state level. Now, in February 1966, he was going to testify before a congressional committee. It looked like a rerun of what had happened before. Even his book wasn't doing the job. In early 1966 it had sold twenty thousand copies, indicating only moderate spread of his ideas. By contrast, Truman Capote's *In Cold Blood* (which, it has been noted, could have been the title of Nader's book) had sold two hundred seventy-nine thousand.

At this point, Nader's good luck entered into the story. He had been noticing that he was being followed by some strange looking characters. He then started getting threatening phone calls. He also found out that people had interviewed his friends, asking whether he was anti-Semitic or homosexual, under the guise that he was being considered for a job. He wasn't being considered for a job and he realized that someone was trying to get information about him to conduct a smear campaign. He had succeeded in raising the salience of *someone*, but who? The obvious culprit was the auto industry. A weaker man or a man with something to hide might just have given up and gone home. But not Nader. This was the chance he was waiting for. He would use the auto industry's harassment of him to raise other people's salience on the auto safety issue.

He contacted Senator Abraham Ribicoff, whose staff Nader had been assisting, and told him what was going on. Ribicoff, concerned about safety, and about snooping, was enraged. Press reports about GM snooping started to appear, Senator Gaylord Nelson denounced GM on the Senate floor, and Ribicoff announced hearings. Nader released the story to the press. A few days later, GM denied most of the story but admitted having conducted an investigation of Nader. Ribicoff, along with Senator Robert F. Kennedy, decided to make GM's spying on Nader an issue at the hearing. The hearing came and, with Nader in the room, James Roche, President of GM, made a public apology to Nader under hostile questioning from Ribicoff and Kennedy. Flashbulbs popped, TV cameras rolled, and suddenly Nader and auto safety became front-page news. The press portrayed Nader as a David slaying Goliath. By proper timing and the use of the media Nader had parlayed hard work, skill, and good luck into heightened salience of auto safety.

> PRINCiple 4.5: The mass media often controls the salience of issues for many actors, and what turns the mass media on is frequently not directly related to the issue.

What was especially fortuitous about these events was that Nader was able to raise salience without antagonizing anyone except those who were already against him. He performed no acts of civil disobedience, threw no bombs, and proposed no radical revision of the American way of life. Instead, he developed the image of a knowledgeable expert who had the American people's interests at heart and was being persecuted by powerful business forces. He became a folk hero for middle America.

As a consequence of increasing the salience of the issue to the American public as well as to members of Congress and the executive branch, Nader, through his impressive show of knowledge, was able to shift the issue positions of the four groups closer to his own views. As their salience for the issue went up and their feeling that Nader was speaking the truth increased, the issue positions of the groups slowly shifted.

Nader was also aided by events concerned with the civil rights and the Vietnam war issues. The riots of the middle 1960s and the growing disillusionment with the Vietnam war tended to make the moderates of both liberal and conservative leanings less hostile toward one another. Instead of directing animosity toward each other, these broad segments of opinion in American society started to question the political leadership. Although auto safety never occupied a position of importance equal to the Vietnam and civil rights issues, the liberals and conservatives found no difficulty in generally agreeing upon the need for change and improvement. Similarly, Congress followed American public opinion and ultimately forced the executive to do the same. Hence, by 1968 the overall issue positions and salience on auto safety were as represented in Chart 4-5.

The chart indicates a substantial improvement over the situation for Nader in 1965. However, the balance was still strongly negative and was by no means settled, primarily because of the large opposition by industry.

Undaunted, Nader began to pursue a new aspect of his strategy. He

CHART 4–5. Issue positions, salience, and power on auto safety by 1968.

	Issue position	Salience	Power	Total
Executive	+1	1	2	+2
Congress	+2	1	2	+4
Industry	−3	3	3	−27
Left wing	+2	1	1	+2
Liberals	+3	2	1	+6
Conservatives	+2	2	2	+8
Right wing	−3	1	1	−3
Total				−8

decided to do no less than reduce the power of big business. (Industry's power, remember, is a key factor in the negative score for auto safety.) He chose two paths, one a very traditional path followed by almost all American social reformers and the other a unique path. The traditional path was to wage a campaign on raising a broad set of antitrust issues for the purpose of increasing executive and congressional power to counteract the power of business. This path has been followed and has produced some success. Its primary difficulty is that the rules and procedures designed to regulate the corporations are administered by people who often come directly out of or go directly back into the industry.

As a concomitant strategy, Nader threatened actually to take over the boards of directors of the auto manufacturers. These boards are elected by the stockholders and Nader used his reputation to get the stockholders to vote for his slate of candidates rather than for management's. He called upon not only ordinary stockholders but the very large stockholders like banks, universities, and churches to support his slate. He started first with General Motors (Project GM). Although even some of the sympathetic stockholders have been wary of installing a pro-Nader governing board, they have been more amenable to vote one consumer representative and specific policy changes in regard to auto safety and GM production. Nader was not fully successful in his first attempts. Nevertheless his increasing votes at annual stockholders' meetings put the GM management under intensive pressure. Nader's strategy was to get GM management to change its issue position on auto safety by threatening to frustrate their fulfilling of a much more important goal—staying in power. Nader in effect was saying: "Make safe automobiles and I'll go away—or keep on making unsafe automobiles and someday I'll have your job." As the last threat began to look more realistic, GM began to change its issue position on auto safety.

PRINCiple 4.6: Changing power sometimes requires
institutional change, which takes a very long time,
but there may be no other alternative.

Since the GM episode Ralph Nader has done much more than improve auto safety. He has created a new page in the history of reform
movements in the United States. Prior to Nader, most attempts to
change laws and policies required the growth of special interest groups
within either of the two major political parties. These special interest
groups did not favor the interests of the majority of the American people. Nader succeeded in generating the idea of public interest groups at
all levels of government to represent the public's interests. These public
interest groups have become important and powerful actors to be considered on all issue areas.

Critics feel that these groups hinder the enactment of any legislation
and will ultimately immobilize the government's functioning. Some
critics also feel that excessive legislation is created by these public interest groups. A frequently cited example was the use of a complicated
warning system to insure that people used their seatbelts for safety. In
the middle 1970s the American public blamed Ralph Nader for those
annoying ringing devices that became mandatory under federal legislation. The tactics of immobilism and excessive legislation are not new to
American politics. Nader and his cohorts may not be blameless in this
respect; but neither are they solely or even primarily responsible.

The responsibility lies in contemporary life's increasing complexity,
which requires laws and policies to encompass this complexity. Ralph
Nader's contribution has been to develop within the capacity of the
American political system a set of actors who will protect the public's
interest. In that respect Nader's work is compatible with the goals of this
book. Only by making everyone a Prince can we initiate responsible
political action at every level of government to insure the quality of life
we all want.

PRINCEtitute CASE #77:
Strategy for the Organization of Widgit-Exporting Countries

5

In the first edition of this book we reported on the activities of a consulting firm called PRINCEtitute, Inc. We told the story of how the organization served as a consultant to the U.S. government on Vietnam policy. PRINCEtitute performed several analyses, concluding that escalation and bombing in Vietnam was not sound policy. Their findings maintained that escalation would simply increase the salience of all the relevant actors within North Vietnam. Instead of deterring them, bombing would make them more resolute in pursuing their objectives. Unfortunately for all concerned, American policymakers did not heed the advice of the PRINCEtitute and followed the escalatory course of action beyond the point of no return.

As the Vietnam war came to its end with the defeat of the United States, there was much gloom in the halls of the PRINCEtitute. The staff knew they could expect no more government contracts in the foreseeable future. They had committed the unpardonable sin of the advisor: to be correct and have your advice ignored.

The PRINCEtitute was therefore forced to turn elsewhere to stay in business. They had to look primarily outside the U.S. for clients because their disfavor with the government made it virtually impossible to obtain work within this country. Unfortunately—and ironically—PRINCEtitute began its overseas operations just at the time when foreigners were becoming hostile toward American business operations, a hostility

45

even further influenced by the revelations that some businesses were serving as cover organizations for U.S. government intelligence operations. Consequently PRINCEtitute began to feel it had no place to turn.

Background to Case #77

Fortunately they were able to develop what turned out to be an extremely profitable contract with a group of foreign governments to help them deal with a foreign policy problem. Their new client was a group of countries whose economies depended to a great extent on their foreign trade income generated by the production and sale of widgit. Widgit is a raw material found in a relatively few places in the world. Those countries fortunate enough to possess large supplies of widgit have found themselves in an extremely beneficial situation, because it has been found that the material, although unpleasant to the sight and the touch, is extremely useful for many different industrial purposes. In fact, the material, which is an unpleasant gray color, is often referred to as "gray gold."

The leaders of the widgit-exporting countries came to the PRINCEtitute because they were puzzled about something. They had all studied economics at the finest European and American universities, and they had learned well the lesson that when demand was high prices go up. However, their experience in government and finance suggested that something was wrong. Over the past several years there had been relatively high demand for widgit among the major purchasers in the West. And yet, in defiance of their economics lessons, the income they received had not risen correspondingly. Not daring to believe that their lessons had been wrong, they had hired some of their former economics professors as advisors to explain the situation to them. The economists, after much research, prayer, and fasting, concluded that prices for widgit had not risen because there were too many suppliers competing with one another. The widgit producers might be excused for thinking they had heard that one before because most of the report came from the Economics I lecture notes of the chief consultant.

Naturally enough, the leaders asked the economists what they could do about the situation. In their formal reply, the economists would only say that nothing could be done about it, that you couldn't repeal the laws of supply and demand. However, our inside information suggests that the economists secretly let slip the hint that if the widgit producers cooperated more and competed less, they would be in better shape. In this way, it was suggested, prices would be more likely to increase.

The leaders naturally asked their advisors how to bring about this coalition. We are fortunate in being able to present the following partial transcript of the conversation between the economists and the client on this point. The conversation was taped by a member of the consulting team, a double agent who, while working as the economist he had been trained to be, had become secretly interested in how people actually made policy decisions. In other words, he had become a "closet Prince," to use the epithet of one of his former colleagues. He eventually wound up supplying this conversation and other information to the PRINCE-titute, where he worked for the rest of his life.

Tape #446–778: economists and
widgit-producing clients

CLIENT: This is all very fine, but how do we bring about this coalition?

ECONOMISTS (after a hurried reading of their dictionaries): We're sorry, but "coalition" is a term of politics and doesn't compute in our models. We are not talking about some artificial institution but about an enduring part of the natural order called a cartel or oligopoly.

CLIENT: So how do we create a cartel?

ECONOMISTS: Pardon us for saying so, but you chaps really are naïve. A cartel isn't something you just go out and create. It arises naturally, out of the economic order of things. And you well know that it's not nice to fool with Mother Economics.

CLIENT: You mean there's nothing we can do about it?

ECONOMISTS: I'm afraid that's right. Well, we've got to catch our plane back to the U.S. By the way, here's our final bill.

* * * *

Needless to say, the client was most disappointed. Fortunately, just at the time that the leaders were feeling most frustrated and in need of some more ideas, one of their representatives met an officer of the PRINCEtitute at their mutual stockbroker. (The PRINCEtitute was selling stock, the leader was buying.) The representative from the widgit-producing country (who interestingly enough had the title of "prince" in his royal family at home) explained the situation to the official. Ever eager to promote world peace (and gain contracts for the PRINCEtitute) the company officer immediately told the prince that it seemed to him that his people's governments were faced with precisely the kind of problem that the PRINCEtitute could help him solve. During lulls in the stock market activity the two men worked out an informal understanding about the outlines of the project. After some further weeks of conversation and correspondence a detailed contract was drawn up for a three-year project. The PRINCEtitute officials had sought a longer contract, but the widgit-producing countries had learned from their experience with economists that they couldn't get their consultants to talk to them until it was close to the time for final payment. They therefore insisted on a shorter contract.

The rest of this chapter details the story of the project. It is based on several sources, including interviews, documents that were more or less freely shown to us as researchers, and the partial transcript of taped conversations among the PRINCEtitute staff. The tapes were made by a concealed recorder that had been installed by the director of the PRINCEtitute and then had been absentmindedly left on for the three-year period that the project ran.

The Initial Stage

The PRINCEtitute staff first had to cope with several problems of cross-cultural communication. The cultural gap was caused not by the nationality differences but by the experience the widgit producers had had with the economists—both when they had been undergraduates and in the recent project. Because of these experiences the clients did not feel comfortable talking about their problems unless they used the supply and demand curves the economists had taught them. In contrast, the PRINCEtitute staff insisted that PRINCE charts were the only path to truth. Eventually the problem was solved by one of the PRINCEtitute's graphic artists. She pointed out that the information in most PRINCE charts could be presented in the format used by economists in talking about supply and demand. A check by the legal section determined that, surprisingly, no economist had taken out a copyright on the curves, and so the staff decided to use them. In this way they were able to convey the information in a form acceptable and understandable to their clients.

For example, Figure 5-1 uses curves to represent the impact of the price of widgit on the behavior of exporters and importers. The vertical axis represents the two groups' respective cohesion, or willingness to cooperate with their own group members. High cohesion (the top of the graph) is the situation of high positive issue position and high salience on the issue of within-group cooperation. Low cohesion (the bottom of the graph) is the situation of neutral or negative issue posi-

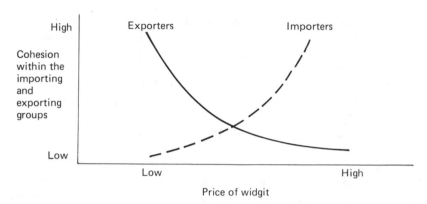

FIGURE 5-1. Price and cohesion curves for widgit exporters and importers.

tion and/or low salience on the issue. In this project, PRINCEtitute had decided not to factor in the power values. Their rationale for this was two-fold: (1) all actors had equal power on the issues in question and (2) the client had been cheap in negotiating the terms of the contract and didn't deserve to be told everything.

The horizontal axis indicates the changing price levels of widgit on the world market. The solid line represents the relationship between price and the exporters' cohesion; the dotted line represents the relationship between price and the importers' cohesion. Cohesion is important because if the widgit-exporting countries try to withhold widgit from the market to force the price up, they will be successful only insofar as every exporting country appears to be willing to withhold widgit. Similarly, if the widgit-importing countries try to stop buying widgit (that is, to organize a boycott), the price will go down only to the extent that the exporting countries believe that importing countries will all support the boycott. To discover the message of this chart, let's follow the transcript of part of the conversation between PRINCEtitute and its client.

Tape #567–934: comments on price and
cohesion curve presentation

CLIENT: I see you've copied one of the figures from the report the economists gave us. Except you labeled it wrong; it should be supply and—

PRINCE: Excuse me, sir. These aren't supposed to be supply and demand curves. I know that's what they look like. But they are actually a picture of a *political* rather than an *economic* situation. As prices go up, there's a decline in

the willingness of you exporters to stick together in bargaining over price. At the same time the importers become more positive about sticking together in their
bargaining with you.

CLIENT: Wait just a minute! You are just telling me about how
oligopolies react to the law of supply and demand. You
expect us to pay all that money for a fancy retelling of
something we learned as freshmen? What is this [ex-
pletive deleted]?

PRINCE: Now don't lose your temper. We're just trying to start
from where you are. I am impressed by your awareness
of the similarities between Figure 5-1 and the familiar
supply and demand curves. However, you can be sure
that we've been doing some hard work for you. In fact,
the powerful PRINCE concepts were used to generate
these charts. Although they begin where an economist
would, you will soon see that there is some additional
information here that will help you solve your problems.

CLIENT: I'm listening.

PRINCE: First, let me show you how the curves in Figure 5-1 are
based on one of the basic PRINCE concepts called
"salience." If you look at Chart 5-1, you will see that
salience on the support of the actions of either coalition
varies according to the price level for that coalition.

CLIENT: What do "OWEC" and "OWIC" mean?

PRINCE: Sorry. OWEC means "Organization of Widgit-Exporting
Countries" and OWIC means "Organization of Widgit-
Importing Countries." The "1," "2," and "3" stand for
any three typical countries in each of the two organizations. As we shall see, there's good reason to think of
the two blocs competing with one another, and with
varying levels of cohesion.

CLIENT: I see. The current price represents an equilibrium point
because the issue positions of each of the countries for
both blocs are identical and the saliences are also the
same. If the price goes down, our OWEC group becomes
stronger. If the price goes up, their OWIC group becomes stronger.

PRINCE: That is exactly right. You obviously have an intuitive
appreciation of PRINCE thinking. As you can see, there
is no way that the price of widgit will increase as long as
the issue positions and salience of the respective countries continue in the relationship that they now have.

CHART 5-1. Salience under varying price levels.

	Issue position on supporting the policy of the group	Salience on issue at		
		10% below current price	Current price	10% above current price
OWEC 1	+3	3	2	1
OWEC 2	+3	3	2	1
OWEC 3	+3	3	2	1
OWIC 1	+3	1	2	3
OWIC 2	+3	1	2	3
OWIC 3	+3	1	2	3

> PRINCiple 5.1: Variation in salience on the same issue for two opposing actors is often interrelated.

CLIENT: Please excuse me for making these impolite observations, but I don't have any "intuitive PRINCE thinking" as you call it. I'm just repeating the conclusions I got from our other consultants.

PRINCE: I understand that. But notice this important difference: They didn't tell you what to do about the situation, except to say that your group must be stronger than the other. Our description of this same situation uses concepts that help point out what you should do in order to achieve your objectives.

CLIENT: I'm very doubtful, but proceed.

PRINCE: What you must do is either reduce the support for a cohesive bloc of importing countries or increase the support for cohesion among your countries. You can do this by changing the issue positions of the country or changing the salience on those issues. There are many ways to change issue position and salience. At this time, my staff back in the U.S. is studying several extremely promising options. Our only problem right now is picking the best of the lot. We'll present it to you in about three weeks.

CLIENT: I'll be waiting.

* * * *

As should be clear from the foregoing conversation, the PRINCEtitute staff member didn't have the foggiest idea what course of action to suggest to the client. He was tempted simply to terminate the contract and so advised his home office. After several long distance telephone calls, however, it was decided that there should be one more meeting with the client to see if something could be worked out. The PRINCE staffer was told to use his best judgment as to whether the contract should be continued or terminated. He was instructed to do whatever he thought was right, and not to be influenced by the fact that his future employment with PRINCEtitute depended upon his successful completion of this project. With this encouraging advice, the staffer held his planned meeting three weeks later.

The Follow-up

Tape #145–743: how to get more OWEC cohesion than OWIC cohesion

CLIENT: I'm anxious to hear the results of your analysis.

PRINCE (to himself): So am I!

CLIENT: I beg your pardon?

PRINCE: Oh, nothing. Now, we have decided to do something more useful than merely give you an answer to your problem. That would be easy enough for us to do, but it wouldn't be in your best long-run interests. So instead, I am going to show you how to use the PRINCE concepts to come up with the answer yourself.

CLIENT: Wow, I haven't heard that one since I took my last liberal arts course in college. So you haven't been able to figure anything out, huh?

PRINCE: Of course we have! (Giggles nervously.) But this way you'll understand it better and in the future you'll be able to apply the concepts to this and other problems. What we have to figure out together is some way to identify another issue. This should be one over which you have control and that doesn't cause dissension among your own countries but does create dissension and confusion among the OWIC bloc. The effect of doing this will be to make the OWIC cohesion less sensitive to the rise in prices. If you remember the curve we originally provided at the outset of this contract, you would be able to move the OWIC curve to the left as indicated by the dotted line in the graph.

FIGURE 5-2.   Effect of generating OWIC dissension on the price
and cohesion curves.

CLIENT: Big deal. You already said that last time. Do you think
by laying economic formats on me, you are going to
make me think that you have helped me? How do I increase dissension within OWIC without increasing it
among ourselves? You've got to quit fooling around.
I've got other policies to worry about. In half an hour
I'm going to a Cabinet meeting on—

PRINCE: That's it. I read in the paper what the Cabinet meeting
will be about. It has to do with the territorial dispute
involving two of your OWEC countries on the one hand,
and a mutual enemy on the other, the latter being an
ally of some of the OWIC group. That's the issue you
can use. Let's call the latter country "I" for purposes of
discussion.

CLIENT: Of course, "I" for—

PRINCE (quickly interrupting): Yes, "I" for "issue." Let's use
that code in case someone is bugging this conversation.
This way, they will not be able to figure out what we
are saying.

CLIENT: All right, let's get back to business. Are you suggesting
that we make a public announcement saying that we are
increasing the price of widgit 20% because the I issue
has not been settled?

PRINCE: Something like that. You could say that OWEC is no
longer willing to sell a commodity as vital as widgit as
long as OWIC allows I to refuse to reach a settlement
with you. Begin by threatening and then implementing a
brief boycott. Later, raise the price 20% and say that it
will be necessary to raise it 20% every three months until the I issue is resolved.

CLIENT: Why go through all that rigamarole if all we really want is to raise the widgit prices?

PRINCE (gaining confidence all the while): It's very simple. If the OWIC countries believe that you are using I as a ploy to justify a raise in prices, they will remain cohesive, and the old patterns will continue. However, if they conclude that the central issue is I and not the price of widgit, they will devote their attention either to resolving I or arguing among themselves over how to resolve I. In any event this will result in a reduction of salience for maintaining cohesion on the issue of widgit price. (Going to the hotel room wall with his can of spray paint in hand.) I can show it clearly with this PRINCE chart. (Chart 5-2).

CLIENT: Why not get to the point? What you mean to say is that there's an inverse relationship between the salience of the price issue and the salience of the I issue. Here, let me have that spray can. The relationship is something like this. (Figure 5-3.)

PRINCiple 5.2: The number of issues an actor can have high salience on is limited; introducing a new high salience issue may reduce the salience on other issues.

PRINCE: It may not be a straight line but it is in that general direction. Moreover, the curves for the OWEC countries is probably in the opposite direction, if you will allow me (Figure 5-4). As salience on I increases, the salience on the price also goes up. So the overall effect will be to make OWEC more cohesive than OWIC.

CHART 5-2. Salience on price levels and I issue if both exist together.

	Salience on supporting widgit policy of OWIC at current price	10% above	Salience on I issue
OWIC 1	2	2	3
OWIC 2	2	2	3
OWIC 3	2	2	3

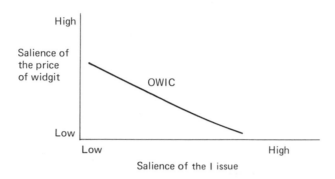

FIGURE 5-3. Salience on widgit prices and on I issue for OWIC.

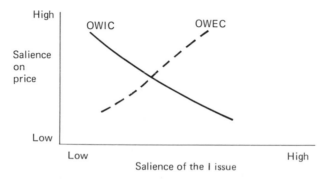

FIGURE 5-4. Salience on widgit prices and on I issue for OWEC and OWIC.

CLIENT: Now the only thing that I have to do is to convince the OWEC governments to go along with the plan.

PRINCE: Yes, we are prepared to help you formulate a strategy for such a purpose.

CLIENT: Are you kidding? Domestic politics is my bag. I scarcely believe we will need your services for that.

PRINCE: But—

CLIENT: I have to get to that Cabinet meeting now. Good day, and thank you very much.

* * * *

Needless to say, PRINCE was ecstatic about the course of the meeting. The staffer had, with the help of the ever reliable PRINCE political accounting system, actually been able to help the client—and also save his own job. He would have been quite satisfied to end the project right there.

But this was not the end of the relationship with the widgit-exporting countries. During the next few months several news accounts appeared about internal dissension and bickering within and between the OWEC countries. PRINCEtitute wasn't surprised, therefore, to receive a call from the client asking for more help. The staffer was dispatched to hold another planning meeting, at which the following conversation took place.

An Urgent Meeting

Tape 151–370: how to get internal support for linking widgit to issue I

CLIENT: It is so nice to see you.

PRINCE: I was hoping that we could meet again. I'm sorry about the trouble you've been having. Why not tell me about it.

CLIENT: Of course. To fill you in, I've prepared my own PRINCE charts. I must confess that your method of making me solve the problems myself was a good idea. It really helped me apply the concepts to this new problem. Consider the situation we face in most OWEC countries (Chart 5–3).

PRINCE: Say, I notice that you have included power in your calculations. I don't believe that we let you, uh, that we found it necessary to include power in our earlier calculations. Where did you pick up that concept?

CLIENT: Don't you remember? You bought me a copy of *Everyman's PRINCE* (first edition) as a farewell gift. I read it with much pleasure and, I believe, enlightenment. Especially so because for the price of your contract I could have bought ten thousand copies. . . .

CHART 5–3. PRINCE charts on the decision to create a crisis on I issue for a typical widgit-exporting country.

	Issue position		Power		Salience		Total
Leader	+1	X	3	X	3	=	+9
OWIC-based corporations	-3	X	1	X	3	=	-9
Bureaucracy	-3	X	3	X	3	=	-27
Extremist factions	+3	X	2	X	3	=	+18
Common people	0	X	1	X	1	=	0
							-9

PRINCE: Yes, uh, why don't you explain those very interesting charts you have prepared.

CLIENT: Very well. As you can see, in the typical OWEC country there is a balance against creating a crisis with respect to issue I. You may wonder why the leaders are only slightly in favor of it and the bureaucracy is against it. The reason is that such a crisis might increase the power of the extremist factions. It might also raise the power and salience of the common people on a lot of issues, and that would be touchy, to say the least, for the ruling groups.

PRINCE: I must say I'm impressed with your grasp of the PRINCE accounting system procedures. In fact, I don't see a single mistake in multiplication or addition. However, I think that although you know the form, you still have some flaws in your techniques of application.

CLIENT: Listen, I didn't come here to be insulted and lectured to.

PRINCE: If I were an economist you'd take it.

CLIENT: You're right. We've paid you as much as them, so go ahead and be patronizing.

PRINCE: The problem is that you have presented the issue incorrectly. It shouldn't be to create a crisis on issue I in isolation, but to get the governments publicly to link issue I to widgit supply and prices. I am sure that if you had done that and assured the various groups (except for the extremists of course) that issue I was really being used to accomplish an increased income, you would have received support from the corporations and the bureaucracy.

CLIENT: I can see your reasoning. We know that the OWIC-based corporations operating on our soil are in favor of higher prices so that they can make windfall profits. Our bureaucrats would go for the idea also. However, you have forgotten a very critical problem that you yourself warned us about earlier.

PRINCE: What's that?

CLIENT: If we openly state that we are using the I issue as a ploy to raise widgit prices, the OWIC countries will stand united against us. Therefore we don't dare tell the OWIC-based corporations or the bureaucracy or even very many of our governmental leaders what our total plan is. That's why the issue is stated the way it is.

PRINCE: Hmm! That is a tough nut to crack. If you'll give us

another contract to study this problem, we'll get back
to you in a couple of months.

CLIENT: Are you kidding me? Do you think that we are going to
give you another contract after you've caused us so
many problems? I'll tell you what. I'll pay you two
more working days.

PRINCE: I guess that's—

CLIENT: But only if you deliver something within two days—
forty-eight hours, not a minute more!

*   *   *   *

Not used to being treated this way, the staffer left the client's office
and went back to his hotel room. He placed a call to PRINCEtitute
headquarters and explained the situation to the duty officer, who said
he would see what he could do. He wasn't very optimistic.

The staffer and the duty officer reviewed all of the cases that they
had dealt with in their years of working for the firm. They agreed that
there were very tricky problems in dealing with salience and especially
in linking salience on different issues. Salience is linked for many different reasons in different situations. The increase in salience for one
actor involved with an issue usually results in the increase in salience for
other actors as well. When this happens with actors who have opposing
issue positions, there is no net effect on the predicted outcome of the
decision at issue. To complicate the matter, there are frequently linkages
across issues. Therefore, when an attempt is made to develop some
trade-off between issues, increasing salience on one issue may not work
because there is likely to be a corresponding increase in salience across
another issue.

The staffer and the duty officer agreed that they were confronted
with the classic salience-linkage problem. They both feared they had
reached a dead-end. The staffer suggested, and the officer agreed, that
one way out would be to cause a rise in salience in such a way that this
rise would appear to be caused by country I. This would make it easy
for the client to institute a policy of connecting widgit to issue I. More
or less in jest, the staffer wished that country I could be provoked into
attacking the two OWEC countries. As the staffer observed, "That
would sure as hell jump up the salience on issue I." A policy of tying
widgit prices to issue I could easily be justified internally and, even
more importantly, would be accepted at face value by the OWIC countries. The duty officer agreed that an attack by I certainly would be
convenient and at that they ended the conversation.

Several hours later the staffer was glumly packing his bags in preparation for his trip back home, certain that he couldn't provide any constructive help for the client. He began to hear much shouting and running on the street below. Looking out his window, he saw that the streets were filled with army vehicles, adding to the confusion and excitement. Quickly checking with the main desk, he learned that a war had begun. The country had been attacked by I, which had simultaneously started war against its neighbors, including two of the most important OWEC members.

Even as he expressed regrets to the desk clerk, the staffer realized what this meant. No matter what the outcome of the war, this was just the thing needed to boost salience on the collateral issue. The staffer well knew what would happen in the next several months. The OWEC leaders first announced a boycott on the export of widgit, which was followed by several price boosts. Given all their concern and the high salience of the I issue, the importing countries were only too willing to pay. Through some miracle the plan had worked.

But was it a miracle? The staffer couldn't help but remember that the duty officer had sounded more reflective than resigned when they had ended their telephone conversation. The staffer knew that the covert operations section of PRINCEtitute had established firm links with many military establishments around the world. But could even they pull off such a coup?

The staffer never found out. Upon returning to an enthusiastic welcome at the PRINCEtitute, he was immediately whisked into a high-level briefing with the PRINCE senior staff. The latter part of that meeting is recorded as follows:

Tape 332-149: final briefing of staffer
on OWEC project

SENIOR:　　This is a fantastic story! I'm sure that we're going to get many more contracts from those people.

STAFFER:　I don't think so, sir, you see, they know the PRINCE technology well enough to apply it to their own problems. In all modesty, I feel they've been taught extremely well. That, plus their own copy of *Everyman's PRINCE*. . . .

SENIOR:　　What! You let them see *Everyman's PRINCE*! Don't you know that damn book is putting us out of business? It tells anyone who reads it how to solve their own political problems. With it, people don't need expert consultants, politicians, or government leaders

to tell them how to make policy. It's downright sub-
versive. Well never mind the deed is done. (Into inter-
com) Williams! See to it that staffer is given six
months' severance pay. He's obviously suited to be an
educator, not a hustler. Staffer, you did a terrific job.
Now get out!

Political Problems of Inflation and Economic Growth

6

For many years now many countries of the world have been faced with an ever-sharpening dilemma in their economic policies. On the one hand, governments attempt to ensure their growing populations the opportunity for jobs and access to resources—in other words, they try to maintain an adequate pace of economic growth. On the other hand, many of the actions governments take to promote growth also contribute to the vicious cycle of inflation.

Making trade-offs between inflation and growth is a public policy similar to many of the other policies discussed in this book. Yet much of the debate assumes that economic policy making is fundamentally different from other types of policy making. The main reason for this is that a special group of experts—economists—play an especially important role in economic policy making. Much of the debate is whether governments are doing what the economists say is the right thing to do. Professional economists, with their masses of data, elegant theories, and complex models, are frequently regarded as the only people capable of defining what the public interest is and how to achieve it.

In this chapter we will take a different approach to some of the problems of economic policy. We are not doubting for a minute (or at least for no more than a minute) the vital information and insight provided by economists. But at the same time we feel that an important insight into the policy process, even this policy process, can be gained from PRINCE-charting some of the policy choices. Let's start with the problem of inflation.

The Politics of Inflation

Inflation, a condition where the price of everything is increasing more than its value, is clearly a political problem, both as to its consequences and its causes. Its political consequences mean that, just like every other policy, it affects different groups in different ways. For example, inflation helps the following groups: people who have debts (because they are repaying their debts incurred at pre-inflation prices with inflated currency), people who have trouble finding jobs—marginal workers (because high inflation usually means more employment), profit-receivers (because profits generally increase faster in times of inflation). At the same time inflation generally hurts the following groups: creditors (because they receive payment for debts at pre-inflation prices), pensioners and others on fixed incomes (because prices generally rise faster than adjustments are made in their incomes), consumers (because they must pay more for everything they buy).

The United States, like almost every other country in the world, has experienced more or less rapid inflation over the past several years. Although there is a good deal of debate about the exact causes of inflation, nearly everyone agrees that government spending generally tends to create inflationary pressures. (We don't mean to give short shrift to an extremely important and complex subject. Government spending doesn't always increase inflation; furthermore, the values of government spending may in many cases outweigh the problems of inflation that it produces. Nevertheless, we feel that our general point is valid.) Governments continue to do things that often result in inflation, so there must be some support for such policies. To see why, let's consider the issue: the government should permit (or at least not oppose) inflation. This is a relevant issue in nearly every country of the world today. But for illustration, let's consider the issue position, power, and salience of some representative groups on this issue. Chart 6–1 provides this information in two categories, one for permitting 5% annual inflation and one for permitting 10% annual inflation. We have taken as the groups those listed above as being either hurt or helped by inflation. Their issue positions are estimated on the basis of how clearly a particular group is helped or hurt. Salience is based on how important the economic gains or losses are to the particular group. Power is estimated according to two considerations: (1) how large the group is and (2) how well organized and coordinated the members of the group are.

As the chart shows, there is a slight positive net support for the lower level of inflation but strong opposition to the higher level. As the rightmost column of the chart indicates, only two groups generate higher scores for the 10% inflation rate. These are debtors and profit-receivers, for whom the issue becomes more salient at the higher level. They are supportive of inflationary policies to begin with, and the higher rates simply make their support more salient.

The opposition of the three groups opposed to 5% inflation increases when the inflation level is 10%. This is especially noteworthy with consumers. The higher levels make their issue position more negative and their salience higher. In addition, the chart indicates an increase in their power because at high levels they will organize into consumer groups and thus lend more weight to the negative scores.

One of the most interesting groups is the marginally employed. Although their issue position and salience change, they remain with the same net score with respect to both levels of inflation. To understand why they show a slight decline in their support for higher inflation we must (however reluctantly) turn to the economists. One of their concepts for studying our problem is what they call a "Phillips curve." A Phillips curve is the means by which economists show the nature of the trade-offs between inflation and employment, which is one of the most important ways of measuring the adequacy of the growth rate. Figure 6-1 presents a Phillips curve approximating the recent performance of the U.S. economy. It shows that up to a point employment does indeed grow along with inflation. It also shows, however, that after inflation exceeds 5% a year, there is very little additional employment gained with higher inflation rates. Hence, the increased economic costs for the marginally employed begin to counterbalance their increased prospects for employment. For that reason, we have estimated that the salience will increase, but the positive issue position will decline, as the annual inflation rate exceeds 5%.

The difficulties of economic choice thus far presented for the various groups—especially for the marginally employed—are clearly mirrored in the difficulties of choice faced by policymakers who must deal with a set of groups such as those portrayed in Chart 6-1. We have made the point that a 5% inflation rate is politically advantageous and a 10% inflation rate is politically harmful. But this leaves two major questions unanswered: (1) What is the inflation rate at which the advantages turn to disadvantages? (2) What groups should a government try to satisfy in choosing an economic policy?

The chart suggests an additional component of the politics of inflation: the imprecision with which economic policy inevitably is implemented and the unavoidable tendency to "overadjust" because of the reliance on group support for policies. The reader might have concluded after the discussion of the Phillips curve that U.S. policymakers need only decide what level of unemployment and inflation they wish and then implement the necessary policy to achieve it. However, this is

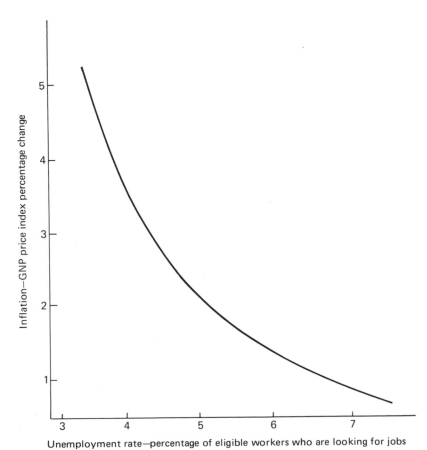

FIGURE 6-1. Phillips curve.

not the case at all. National policymakers deal with a situation in which local officials, businesspeople, labor groups, and many others inside and outside the territory of the United States can make adjustments in their policies that could lead to actions that counteract the policies taken by the U.S. government. Moreover, the economic instruments are imprecise and even the economists' crystal ball is quite cloudy. Therefore even when relying on expert opinion, officials cannot be sure when a certain action is insufficient, just adequate, or an overreaction.

The rather large jump from positive to extremely negative balance concerning inflation shown in Chart 6-1 also indicates the group pressure that can lead governments to overreact. The ideal economic policy, some might argue, would be one that relied exclusively on the consensus of experts and responded to perceived problems with con-

CHART 6-1. Responses to the issue of allowing inflation by the government.

Actors	5% annual inflation				10% annual inflation				Group differences for two levels of inflation
	Issue position	× Power ×	Salience	= Total	Issue position	× Power ×	Salience	= Total	
Profit-receivers	+2	2	1	+4	+2	2	3	+12	+8
Debtors	+2	1	1	+2	+2	1	2	+4	+2
Marginal workers	+2	2	1	+4	+1	2	2	+4	0
Creditors	-2	2	1	-4	-3	2	3	-18	-14
Fixed-income-receivers	-2	1	1	-2	-3	2	3	-18	-16
Consumers	-1	1	1	-1	-3	3	3	-27	-26
			Total	+3			Total	-43	

tinuous "fine tuning" or immediate and marginal adjustments of spending, taxation, and other policies to obtain a desired mixture between growth and inflation. If experts were really as expert as they liked to believe, and if policies didn't have to affect real people, such a procedure might be possible. But unfortunately such conditions don't exist outside of the economics textbooks. Policies must be made by getting bureaucracies to decide on something, by persuading Congress to pass a law, by reacting to consumer groups that suddenly organize and activate themselves, and by many other sudden human pressures and obstacles that do not subject themselves to the fine tuning recommended by experts. (Notice how in Chart 6-1 the increase in salience and power by consumer groups causes a tremendous change in the pressure on economic policy.)

Part of the overadjustment is for economic reasons. Once an inflationary or deflationary trend begins there is a tendency for it to get out of hand. With this knowledge in mind, governmental leaders have overreacted in the past. But much of the overadjustment is political because by the time a large enough group of people realize that inflation is about to become runaway, an anti-inflationary policy becomes politically powerful. People's tendency at first to underreact and then to overreact as individuals is amplified in groups generally and in political bodies specifically. This can be explained in PRINCE terms. As inflation becomes the big problem, the salience and sometimes the power of those most negatively affected increases rapidly. As unemployment increases rapidly, the salience and power of those most affected increases radically. The tendency exists for extreme governmental actions as either inflation or unemployment becomes more pronounced.

PRINCiple 6.1: When there are many competing interests focused on a single public policy, changes in
policies tend to occur too late and be too extreme.

Limiting Economic Growth

Over the past few years scholars, headline writers, and other prophets have raised the grim prospect of a future world so overpopulated, under-nourished, polluted, and devoid of resources that it could not survive. Depending on the degree of pessimism, these writers have predicted the destruction of the human race sometime within the next half century and the next five hundred years. Such warnings are not new. Ever since the beginning of history there have been those saying that their civiliza-tion was about to destroy itself for one reason or another: too little prayer, too many children, or whatever action or inaction a particular doom-sayer most disliked.

Over the past decade these varied fears have been integrated into a generalized policy position: opposition to "excessive" economic growth. This argument has received especially strong impetus from the recent appearance of a book entitled *The Limits to Growth* by Donella H. Meadows, et al. (New York: Universe, 1972). In many wasy *The Limits to Growth* is merely one more voice crying against thoughtless eco-nomic growth. What is different about this book, however, is that it bases its arguments on a set of explicit assumptions and data that are formalized into a computer program that projects the future course of population, pollution, resource depletion, and other crucial indicators of the human condition. Many critics have claimed to find faults with various aspects of the analysis the authors present, but at least they have made explicit their assumptions and have graphically demon-strated the results of alternative projections of the future.

In *The Limits to Growth* and other arguments about the subject, however, there is, we feel, the same kind of narrowness that pervades other debates on economic policy. This is the assumption that the way to bring about desirable change is to argue more persuasively—with data, theory, models, and whatever else may help—as to the desirability and even necessity of a particular course of action. Few, if any, of the arguments of this debate have looked at the political forces underlying current policies relating to growth and its limitation. We feel that this set of policies, no less than policies relating to inflation, should be looked at from the political, as well as the economic, perspective.

> PRINCiple 6.2: No matter how technical the public question, political factors must be considered important.

As we shall point out, there is at least one good reason for the growth-limiters to avoid consideration of the political factors. This reason is that the political forces today are overwhelmingly stacked up against any possibility of limiting growth. Despite all the rational arguments and prophecies of doom, the weight of dominant political forces is in favor of expanding, rather than limiting, growth.

To illustrate why this is so, consider a hypothetical three-person decision-making body. It may be a local legislature, a national legislature, a government agency, or an international organization. The basic dynamics will remain the same. We will call the three members Trucker, Goodwill, and Hawk. We will assume that there are three issues to be decided: (1) build more roads, (2) provide more social welfare, and (3) provide more military defense.

We will assume that each of the three has read *The Limits to Growth*, or has been otherwise exposed to the arguments opposing economic growth, and has been impressed with such arguments and is thus opposed to unnecessary growth and spending. In fact each is opposed to spending in all but his own particular area of interest. This means that two of the three are opposed to each of the spending proposals before the decision-making body. The problem is that the only thing they really care about (have high salience for) is their own particular issue. Thus we have the situation presented in Chart 6-2. Each proposal is, in the abstract, opposed by two of the three members. Yet the net political support scores are positive for all three. The reason, of course, is that the one actor with positive issue position on each issue also is the only one with high salience. (We have assumed that power is equal on all issues among the three actors.)

This seemingly paradoxical situation is actually a fairly common occurrence in legislatures and other decision-making bodies. "Everyone" wants to protect the environment, cut down on spending, and prevent excessive growth. And yet the only thing they really have high salience on is the thing they favor.

Furthermore, Chart 6-2 is based on the conservative and unrealistic assumption that no bargaining or coalition formation takes place among

CHART 6-2. PRINCE charts on three spending issues.

Actors	More roads				More welfare				More defense			
	Issue position	Power	Salience	= Total	Issue position	Power	Salience	= Total	Issue position	Power	Salience	= Total
Mr. Trucker	+3	3	3	+27	-3	3	1	-9	-3	3	1	-9
Mr. Goodwill	-3	3	1	-9	+3	3	3	+27	-3	3	1	-9
Ms. Hawk	-3	3	1	-9	-3	3	1	-9	+3	3	3	+27
				+9				+9				+9

the actors. If the actors have a reasonable expectation that the total spending budget will be large enough to support their own project as well as the projects of others, the friendship-neutrality-hostility chart among them would contain all plus signs (as in Chart 6-3). In other words, if there is an expectation of a large budget, especially if the budget has been large in the past, there will be a tendency for the issue positions to converge on supporting the actor who has high salience for each issue. All issue positions will become positive on all issues, so the prospect of high spending will be increased.

PRINCiple 6.3: As long as resources increase, political support can be maintained by adopting public policies that satisfy the most salient interest of each actor.

Consider the forces now operating on the United States government. Few political forces actually work to limit economic growth policies. To demonstrate the absence of political forces, we have performed another PRINCE analysis. Chart 6-4 reveals that only those groups associated with environmental concerns would maintain a consistent position supporting the slowdown of economic growth within the United States. Businesspeople, labor, and the consumer certainly would not.

Outside the United States, most international organizations such as the World Bank or even the International Monetary Fund would support moderate economic growth but countries of Europe, North and South America, and Asia would feel an economic threat if the United States slowed down its economic growth substantially. Even the communist countries would be interested in keeping the American economy expanding because that condition will help them develop and maintain their economic growth.

CHART 6-3. Friendship-neutrality-hostility chart among three members of a hypothetical decision-making body under conditions of large spending budget.

	Trucker	Goodwill	Hawk
Trucker	X	+	+
Goodwill	+	X	+
Hawk	+	+	X

CHART 6-4. Mini-PRINCE chart on limiting economic growth in the U.S.

Actor	Issue position	Power	Salience	Total
U.S. business	-3	3	3	-27
U.S. labor	-2	2	3	-12
U.S. consumer	-1	2	2	-4
U.S. environmental groups	+3	1	3	+9
World bank	-1	1	3	-3
International monetary fund	-1	1	1	-1
Western countries	-1	2	2	-4
Communist countries	-2	1	1	-2
Developing countries	-3	1	2	-6
				-50

The evidence is fairly clear that increasing economic growth will be followed as a general policy. There will be some conditions, of course, in which the policy will momentarily reverse for short-term adjustments to inflation. These conditions were discussed in the previous section of this chapter. However, in the long-term, the pressures against economic growth as a conscious governmental policy seem extremely weak. We might point out that similar pressures exist in virtually every country in the world so that as a whole the world will have trouble limiting its economic growth.

This is not to say that decisions are not taken that will have a limiting effect on growth. On the contrary, we saw in the previous section in this chapter how our national leaders will frequently develop a deflationary policy by limiting governmental spending. Other instances may be cited, such as the decision made in the early 1970s with respect to the conservation of energy and the elimination of pollution. At the local level, citizen groups are frequently able to protect certain areas from economic development through zoning laws.

For the most part, however, actions taken to limit economic growth are highly specific and usually bound by time, space, or subject-matter. Hence, the antipollution laws were aimed at industrial and utility plants' burning of coal and at the automobile's burning of oil-based products. A general policy calling for the reduction in energy expenditures to the extent that it would slow down economic growth was never developed. Moreover, as the oil shortage imposed by the boycott of oil by the Organization of Petroleum Producing Countries took its effect, many of the antipollution laws were softened and plans for maintaining economic growth while reducing the use of oil were developed.

Attempts by the United States government to curtail economic growth occur only after a runaway inflation seriously threatens or actually begins. Again the policies are not aimed primarily at limiting economic growth but merely at limiting inflation. As soon as the inflation appears to be contained within what is considered to be acceptable limits, the growth policies are resumed.

At the state and local levels, there may be instances when economic development is limited or even prohibited. However, this serves to push the economic development efforts into other areas. For most local units of government, economic growth is never curtailed throughout its entire territory of jurisdiction. Consequently, the forces of economic development may have to relocate, if not within that particular locality, at least to some place nearby. Rarely is the absolute rate of growth affected by these policies.

The reason for this overall urge to develop economically is political. All actors wish to gain as much in economic payoffs as they can. In making decisions, governments that do not generate an ever-increasing pie of economic benefits will have to disappoint some, if not all, groups. The easiest course to follow is to increase the resources available rather than force decisions that will have direct and short-run heavy costs. Governments do this by promoting economic growth.

The argument that arises from this political fact is whether or not there is a set of conditions that at some point will make it impossible for a society or the world as a whole to increase the total size of the pie. Those cited at the beginning of this section argue that there is a "limit to growth" and that we are rapidly approaching that limit. They see the limit as a result of the increasing size of the population and the increasing costs in natural resources to sustain that population. In addition to calling for strict controls on population growth, these people argue that our consumption of goods and services that require natural resources and environmental pollution must be contracted, if not checked.

Some argue that technological breakthroughs render the limits cited by the pessimists less constraining. They point to the fact that pessimists have been making similar arguments for years but have overlooked either the capacity of people to change their behavior or the technological breakthroughs that allow us to produce more food with fewer resources.

To further complicate the matter, there is the fact that for many people of the world the argument that we are consuming too much is meaningless. Individuals suffering poverty whether in rich or in poor countries are not concerned with the earth's limits to growth. Instead, they are worried about feeding themselves. Some even see the call for population control and for a limit to their growth as politically motivated by the rich and the powerful to keep the poor and weak under their control. Hence, although upper-class Americans may find the limits–

to–growth argument persuasive, lower-class urban dwellers around the globe consider the argument to be a cover for the maintenance of the status quo.

> PRINCiple 6.4: The poorer the actor, the higher the salience on growth issues.

For a number of reasons, then, the political forces fostering economic growth are much stronger than those that would limit that growth on a systematic basis. In terms of our PRINCE analysis, there are too many actors with too much power and salience opposing the broadscale limiting of economic growth either in the United States or throughout the globe. The solution, of course, would be for the strengthening of actors who can counter balance those in favor of growth. This was the thinking behind the decision to establish the U.S. Environmental Protection Agency. It is also behind Nader's efforts, described in Chapter 4, to build strong public interest groups. But private and public actors continue to be overwhelmed by the forces at home and abroad favoring continued and rapid economic growth. Institutions and groups that can make the case that we are reaching our economic growth limits must develop if economic growth is ever to be limited.

Bobby Planter vs. The Bureaucrat: A PRINCE Analysis

7

There once was a very bright young Ph.D. named Bobby Planter who went to work for the Department of Housing of the State of California. Dr. Planter began his job one Monday morning in August of 1969. He had just received his Ph.D. in modern housing, an exciting and innovative interdisciplinary program offered by Southern State Normal University. Planter had graduated *cum laude* from Harvard with a B.A. in economics in 1966 and had chosen SSNU because it had the best (not to mention the only) Ph.D. program in modern housing. His curriculum had drawn upon the departments of economics, geography, bricklaying, public administration, and law. All his coursework and research (including a dissertation) were focused on one concern—delivering better housing for less money to Americans, especially poor Americans.

The night before Planter was to start working he was paid a visit by Dr. Lyle Stuart, also a young Ph.D., who was leaving the Department of Housing. Dr. Stuart was moving to greener pastures by taking a job with the Department of Urban Planning in Little Rock, Arkansas. After a few drinks, Stuart told Planter that the California Department of Housing was filled with typical bureaucrats who, as anyone knows, are afraid of their own shadows and who talk in incomprehensible riddles filled with uninterpretable jargon. Stuart recounted at least a dozen instances when he had identified the proper strategy to solve a particular problem but was thwarted by the bureaucrats' overconcern with the politicians, the public, the budget, and their superiors. He illustrated in graphic terms how every suggestion he made was ignored, treated as an "interesting recommendation," or viewed as an occasion for a study committee.

> PRINCiple 7.1: Bureaucrats have to operate in a situation in which their power is low.

Of course, Planter had already expected this. His public administration professor at SSNU was a brilliant thirty-year-old full professor who had attained wisdom during a six-month career in government. He taught his students the latest in administrative techniques, including cost-benefit analysis and permanent sensitivity training. This professor had unsuccessfully tried to organize a graduate public administration program at SSNU, had failed to implement his administrative training practices in several state governments, and had been frustrated in an attempt to reorganize the curriculum of public administration at SSNU. In fact, there was probably no one within a thousand miles whose failures in dealing with bureaucracies made him so well qualified to teach public administration.

This expert professor could describe in great detail the conservatism and imbecility of bureaucrats, and he thoroughly tested his students, including Planter, on their ability to understand the "bureaucratic condition." Hence, Planter was well prepared for his job—which is to say that he expected the worst. Stuart's visit only served to reinforce Planter's expertise on the nature of modern bureaucracy.

During the first week of his job, Planter discovered (with some unhappiness—and a great deal of relief) that the interpretation supplied by his public administration professor and confirmed by Stuart was absolutely correct. He confirmed his notions by using the world-famous participant-observation techniques developed at SSNU ("snooping with a moral purpose," as his public administration professor had called it). For example, Planter witnessed an assistant to Harvey Lowe, the head of the Department of Housing, refuse to approve a trip by a departmental employee to Los Angeles to investigate housing problems on the grounds that the mayor of Los Angeles would consider it meddling. "Better people should live in rat-infested housing than the mayor should be a little ruffled," thought Planter.

From that time on, Planter resolved to do his share to rectify at least one obvious cause of malaise in the United States: incompetent public administration. The opportunity to carry out his pledge was not long in coming. In the second week of September, Harvey Lowe announced that the very next week there would be a high-level departmental meeting to discuss how to encourage the use of more efficient home-building methods and materials in the Los Angeles area. Planter was especially eager for this meeting. He had written his Ph.D. dissertation on the use of new building methods and materials in Plattsburg, New York. So he was sure he could use his expertise effectively to intervene at the meeting and begin to change the archaic bureaucratic processes that dominated the Department of Housing.

He labored all weekend to develop a comprehensive plan to promote the use of new building techniques and materials in Los Angeles. He studied the building codes, the local and state laws, the existing practices, and the nature of businesses and unions in the local construction industry. He relied upon all the interdisciplinary skills he had developed at SSNU. He certainly would have received at least an A– from the director of the Ph.D. program in modern housing.

The meeting started fifteen minutes late because the deputy chief of the department was slow in brewing the coffee. The delay only served to strengthen Planter's resolve. Finally, Lowe opened the discussion by identifying the problem. He said there was some evidence that a three-bedroom house could be built and sold at a reasonable profit for about $22,000 if all of the newest techniques and materials were used. He continued by estimating that given the kinds of materials and techniques presently in use, the best price for a comparable house in the Los Angeles area was $29,000. The primary reason for the meeting was to develop a strategy to bring the prices of houses closer to the lower figure.

Planter took the floor as soon as Lowe finished speaking. First, he pointed out that his calculations led him to believe the gap was wider— $21,000 using the new techniques versus $32,000 using existing methods. Nevertheless, even if Lowe were correct (which in Planter's mind was highly doubtful because Lowe had majored in English literature rather than in modern housing), something had to be done. Planter continued by saying that the situation was deplorable given the available technologies. He advocated a concerted attack on the problem through the following actions:

1. A public statement by the governor calling for more efficient methods and materials in the housing industry
2. The establishment of a uniform state-wide set of building codes based upon the guidelines set by the federal government's Department of Housing and Urban Development
3. A $300,000,000 program to train contractors and skilled laborers in the use of the new techniques and materials
4. The creation of a watchdog committee to monitor building in the Los Angeles area. This committee would be staffed

by local citizens—consumers—and members of the State Housing Department. Its job would be to identify publicly those builders who refused to adopt the new methods and procedures.

Planter presented his arguments with perfectly constructed charts and graphs. He projected that by following his plan it would be reasonable to expect that within two years the average cost of a three-bedroom house would be down approximately to $24,000 (this sum represents adjustment for the inflationary dollar).

Planter looked around him as he finished his talk and saw that the group was visibly stunned. The other six members, including Lowe (who had by now consumed four cups of coffee), sat nervously listening. It seemed to Planter several minutes before anyone spoke. The first person to break the silence was the same assistant who had refused to sign the travel authorization the first week Planter was there. He was a fifty-year-old man who giggled nervously and was extremely polite— the kind of guy you would never want to borrow money from. His name was Mortimer LaStrange, and he had been born a bureaucrat.

PRINCiple 7.2: Technical knowledge must be used skillfully before it can give power to political actors.

LaStrange started out by congratulating Planter for prividing such a stimulating program of ideas. He was so impressed with the ideas that he proposed the immediate establishment of an interdepartmental committee from the half-dozen or so agencies that LaStrange identified as being concerned with Planter's proposed course of action. This committee could thoroughly explore the merits of Planter's ideas, said LaStrange, and, in his giggling words, "do some fine tuning on our young friend's already fine thoughts."

At first, Planter was pleased and more than a little surprised. However, the impact of the flattery soon wore off, and he remembered what his public administration professor and Lyle Stuart had told him. "My God!" he said to himself. "Here we go again, using committees to kill innovative ideas." LaStrange continued even while Planter was trying to recover. He argued in his beautiful bureaucratic style that the problem was "multifaceted" and that a large number of private and public interests were involved. He suggested that an advisory commission be set up with members drawn from various groups including the Los Angeles mayor's office, local union and construction industry groups, companies producing the new techniques and methods, and members of the Housing Department. This committee would make recommendations to Lowe relating to the issues raised by Planter after a thorough study. He proposed that the committee be called "The Southern California Ad Hoc Advisory Commission on Building Methods in Housing and Other Construction."

By now Planter was horrified. He had witnessed first-hand the incredible stupidity of bureaucrats; worse yet, he had seen the perversion of his own carefully framed ideas. Planter was even more crushed when, before he could reply, Lowe excused himself from the room, saying either that he had to talk with the governor or had to play golf (Planter wasn't sure which) and placing LaStrange in charge of the meeting. His final words were that "Mortimer seems to have everything under control." Although Planter had not been in the bureaucracy long enough to be infected with the common disease of paranoia, he did start to wonder whether LaStrange and Lowe had previously discussed the matter and if they were secretly conniving with the building industry and the unions.

Bobby Planter and Mortimer LaStrange have presented two sharply contrasting styles for lowering the cost of housing. Bobby's method is to launch a frontal attack on the vested interests that profit from the high cost of construction, including the men in power, frequently in local communities, who tacitly accept industry practices that are costly to the consumer. LaStrange's plan, from Planter's point of view, reeked of compromise from the very start. LaStrange first proposed the establishment of a study committee, which is a time-honored device to slow down action (while people have to wait for the study committee to do its studying) and also greatly increases the chances of watering down the proposed action by compromise (because the delay and the forum of the study committee will increase the chances of conflicting points of view being effectively put forward). The advisory commission will tend toward the same outcomes, plus some additional ones equally distasteful from Planter's viewpoint. The advisory commission was to be composed of labor and business groups that would undoubtedly be hostile to the proposed policy. This device, bringing in opponents of a policy to help plan it, is as old as bureaucracies. It has a name: cooptation. It is based on the principle, which usually holds true, that people who are associated with the early stages of policy making—especially on an "insider" basis—are very likely to be in favor of the policy, or at least moderate in their opposition. Once again, of course, the price paid for such a strategy is dealing, compromise, and the inevitable tailoring of policy, to some degree at least, in the direction of the groups engaged as advisors.

> PRINCiple 7.3: Cooptation is a strategy required when one is dealing with more powerful actors.

Which strategy is better, the head-on confrontation of the radical innovator or the slow and easy probings of the old-time bureaucrat? A simple and reasonable question, but one that is never answered in the actual world of daily politics. The reason it is never answered is that human beings can't experiment by trying competing solutions to the same political problems: Trying one solution always changes the situation and the problem. The psychologists can put rats through different mazes under different conditions of reward and punishment to see what happens, but human situations cannot be treated this way. (If for no other reason than no one has yet put up the money to build mazes big enough to fit humans.)

However, this is no longer a problem. PRINCE, if not quite the better mousetrap, does in fact serve as a simulated maze through which we can symbolically make the actors in our story run. The first time through we will set up our simulated maze in the way that LaStrange preferred it; after that we will run the players through according to Bobby Planter's wishes. And finally, we will dredge up our old friends, the PRINCE charts, to show why the people involved scurry through their little paths as they do.

LaStrange's Maze*

LaStrange was appointed chairman of The Southern California Ad Hoc Advisory Commission on Building Methods in Housing and Other Construction. This commission was organized after several meetings of the interdepartmental committee where the time was taken up almost exclusively by exchanges of ever-decreasing cordiality between Planter and LaStrange. Despite their differences, LaStrange invited Planter to be on the commission, along with an old bureaucratic hack who had once been an elected official of a labor union; these three represented the Department of Housing. LaStrange also appointed the legislative assistant of a Los Angeles area state senator who was suspected of re-

---

*As you might suppose, the authors, being academics, did not write most of this book. Wherever possible, we assigned term papers that could be turned into appropriate chapters. However, the following sections were drafted while graduate students were on their annual spring Beer Bust and Rally Against Inequality and thus were unavailable. Consequently, we fed the numbers from the PRINCE charts into a computer, which produced the following two scenarios.

ceiving large donations from construction companies. In addition, he appointed a member of the Los Angeles mayor's staff, a local building trade union leader, and the owner of the biggest construction company in the area. Finally, LaStrange recruited the vice-president of Kwiki Homes, Inc., a leading supply company in developing more efficient building materials and techniques.

The first meeting took place in February of 1970. In a series of successive monologues each individual said his piece about the housing industry in the Los Angeles area. The union official and the owner of the construction company complained about governmental interference in private enterprise. The mayor's assistant said that the building codes and practices were really a matter that the local building inspectors could handle. Planter chastised the construction industry and the building unions for their reactionary attitudes and their disregard of the consumer. The legislative assistant said that the state should do more for the building industry and promised his senator's support of building subsidies and more liberal home loans. Finally, the vice-president from Kwiki Homes, Inc. talked about exciting new techniques and materials that could revolutionize home building, increase both productivity and profits, and provide a demand for more skilled labor.

By the time the speeches were complete, there was little time left for a discussion of what the committee should do. The muted threats of the local businessman, labor, and the mayor's assistant that the committee should be eliminated were covered up by a coughing spell LaStrange developed right after the speech of the mayor's assistant. LaStrange simply assumed that there was going to be a second meeting and suggested a date. After an hour's hassling over the time and place of the next meeting, there was agreement and the first meeting ended.

The second meeting was different from the first. Most of the members of the committee began calling each other by their first names, and except for Planter were quite friendly. As they entered the room, a janitor was placing a 16-mm projector on a table in front of a screen. LaStrange started the meeting by explaining that the vice-president from Kwiki Homes, Inc. had brought a film explaining the new techniques and materials. Although it was not on the agenda, LaStrange inquired whether or not it would be appropriate to start the meeting by watching the film. Planter objected on the grounds that it was an attempt to slow down the work of the committee. But LaStrange ignored him and went right on talking. The vice-president—whom Planter considered an ally—gave him such a stare that he stopped protesting. Also, the projector and screen were placed so that one person had no seat. This meant that if the film were not shown right away, the projector and screen would have to be completely put away.

> PRINCiple 7.4:   Discuss procedure when there are strong
> differences among participants on a committee.

Everyone was impressed by the content of the film, particularly the owner of the construction firm. There was a spirited discussion of how these techniques and approaches could be more fully exploited in the Los Angeles area. A proposal was developed to establish a set of objectives that local and state government, business, and labor could simultaneously pursue. However, time ran short before there was any definition of specific objectives.

The third meeting was never held. Everyone but LaStrange and the other bureaucratic hack said he could not make it. Planter boycotted the meeting to show his displeasure at its slow pace, and the other people said they had more pressing business. In spite of what Planter perceived to be the failure of LaStrange in strategy, the following events took place:

1. By the end of 1971, minor revisions in local housing codes were implemented to allow the use of some of the newer materials and techniques.
2. For the first time in history the price of a three-bedroom house in the Los Angeles area did not rise during a twelve-month period (June 1970–July 1971).
3. A modest increase in the production of low-cost housing had occurred in the Los Angeles area during 1971.

> PRINCiple 7.5: If the purpose of a committee is to
> educate its members so they will change their
> issue position, the death of the committee might
> represent success.

In addition, LaStrange had submitted a report of the commission (produced totally by his staff) calling for small grants to help retrain workers in the use of the new materials and techniques. This report became the basis for legislation submitted by the senator whose legislative assistant had been on the commission. Although there was still a great gap between the real and the ideal in the price of building a three-bedroom house, LaStrange had helped to create some conditions for ultimate improvement.

Planter's Maze

Bobby Planter began by drafting a public statement to be issued by the governor's office. The statement called for improvement in the productivity of the housing industry. The speech was to be made at a special news conference and publicized as widely as possible. When the governor's staff assistant—who was an undergraduate intern—was approached with the proposal, he told Planter that he ought to take some more political science courses—or maybe take his first one. Why, he said, should the governor spotlight the ills of that particular industry? It was not his role to increase the productivity of industries. The intern said that he wouldn't even send the request to the governor. Planter tried, with no success, to talk to someone else in the governor's office. (When Planter complained to Lowe about the incident, Lowe fumed about the incompetence of the governor's staff and promised to look into the matter. Needless to say, Planter never heard anything of it again.)

PRINCiple 7.6:   Access to actual actors is often difficult.

Undaunted, Planter developed a uniform state-wide building code and showed it to the legislative assistant of California's most liberal state senator. The assistant told Planter that although his boss thoroughly approved of the idea, it would never get through the legislature because the power of the building industry and labor unions was so great. Moreover, the local municipalities would fight the move. As a result, there was no cooperation in the legislative branch.

The proposal for a large program to educate contractors and retrain laborers was rejected as premature at every point in the government. Such a program without federal subsidy had no chance of success during the period of tight state budgets that characterized the early 1970s. Moreover, many people questioned the idea of a program that would subsidize those building industries that were producing newer products and techniques. The fact that the questioning emanated from those lobbies that were supported by older building firms and by labor made little difference. There was, consequently, no attempt at legislation of this type.

Finally, the proposal for a watchdog committee to enlist consumer pressure on the building industry was rejected by Harvey Lowe. Lowe's compulsive desire to avoid confrontations of any sort led him to tell Planter that although the idea was sound, there were "constraints operating to limit its feasibility" (a bureaucratic phrase meaning "I'm scared to do it"). There was no development of any type of committee that would generate communication among the interested parties.

By this time, Planter was convinced that it was impossible to get the needed action by the California bureaucracy. His plans were obviously rejected because the bureaucrats were too insecure and too jaded to try anything new, he thought. For that reason, when the University of Southeastern Alaska's Department of Urban Housing offered him a professorship (at a salary 50 percent higher than what he was getting from California) he resigned his post in the Housing Department. Sitting in the airport waiting for his flight to Ketchikan, Planter read the newspaper. One story that caught his eye was headlined:

HOME PRICES UP 10% OVER LAST YEAR

The Two Styles Compared

The skilled student of PRINCE should already have begun to understand the reasons for Planter's failure and LaStrange's ability to produce, if not spectacular success, at least something more than failure. Planter ignored every implication of the PRINCE system; LaStrange followed those implications as if by instinct.* To check on how accurate your guesses are (which is to say how close your guesses are to the authors'), let's briefly look at the strategies of the two men in PRINCE terms.

We will examine the issue position, power, and salience of the actors for the issue of improving cost-efficiency in the building industry of Los Angeles. Chart 7-1 indicates that the overall net opposition to the issue comes primarily from the labor unions. The second most powerful group, the building industry, is not totally convinced that it would be in its interest to push for low-cost methods. It is also apparent that the lack of power and salience among the governor, the mayor, and the consumer makes their positions rather peripheral.

The friendship-neutrality-hostility patterns among the actors must also be taken into account. Chart 7-2 illustrates three basic divisions among the actors. First, there is the split between local and state governmental units with the former being extremely suspicious of the latter.

---

*We are speaking figuratively, of course. There is as yet no definitive evidence from ethological or biological research that conclusively proves that any members of *homo sapiens* are actually born with instinctive PRINCE capabilities. See, however, "Nature vs. Nurture and PRINCE: Evidence from Planarian Earthworms and College Sophomores," *American PRINCE Science Review* 2 (September 1971): 80-96.

CHART 7-1. Issue position, salience, and power for improving building productivity in Los Angeles.

Actor	Issue position	Salience	Power	Total for each actor
Housing Department	+3	3	1	+9
Governor	+1	1	2	+2
Mayor of Los Angeles	+1	1	3	+3
Building industry	-1	3	2	-6
Labor	-2	3	3	-18
Consumer	+3	1	1	+3
		Total for the issue		-7

CHART 7-2. Friendship-neutrality-hostility chart.

This actor	Feels about this actor					
	Housing department	Governor	Mayor of Los Angeles	Building industry	Labor	Consumer
Housing department	X	–	+	+	+	+
Governor	+	X	–	+	–	+
Mayor of Los Angeles	–	–	X	+	+	+
Building industry	–	+	+	X	–	+
Labor	–	–	–	–	X	–
Consumer	+	–	+	–	–	X

Second, there is the split between the private groups and the government. This split more clearly involves the Housing Department against business and labor rather than the governor's and mayor's office. Third, there is hostility between the building industry and labor.

Everything Planter did was designed to force the building industry and labor unions to alter their positions through political pressure from the state government. The plan to get the governor to take a firm public stand, to use the state legislature to shape the behavior of business and labor through coercion (uniform laws) and bribes (training grants) and the use of a consumer-dominated watchdog committee were highly visible and straightforward methods to change the way houses were built.

What Planter failed to understand was that the state government had neither the power nor the salience to do very much. Nor could he realistically expect a consumer revolt or even a significant consumer pressure campaign to occur. Moreover, given the hostility of the mayor's office, labor, and the building industry to governmental intervention from the state, Planter's plan could only increase antagonism.

The consequence of Planter's ideas would have been to bring business and labor together in alliance with the local governmental officials to resist the efforts of the Housing Department. The use of high-salience techniques would have created conditions under which business and labor would have forgotten their basic antagonisms and joined together. Nor could there have been much increase in the strength among consumer groups and the governor's office. Given the political structure portrayed in the charts, there was little hope that a coalition among the Department of Housing, the governor, the mayor, and the consumer could have formed or been effective. The governor, the Housing Department head, and members of the state legislature were well versed in the PRINCE system, so it is not surprising that Planter could not get them to accept his strategy for action.

In contrast, LaStrange clearly understood the constraints imposed by limited salience or power for those actors other than the building industry and the labor unions. His understanding led him to devise a strategy that gave the two powerful forces sufficient representation on a committee that was clearly low-profile. A thorough study of the committee illustrates LaStrange's strategy. First, the length of the name of the commission along with the inclusion of such innocuous items as "Ad Hoc" and "Housing and Other Construction" and "Southern California" served further to insure that its activities would be kept on the back pages of the local newspapers. In fact, LaStrange kept the profile so low that the news media never reported much of anything that the committee was doing.

Although people make fun of the jargon and ponderous ways of the bureaucrats, it is the bureaucrats who often have the last laugh. Jargon is like a coat of armor protecting them from politicians and the public so that they can get things done. In this particular case LaStrange's use of such a long title for the committee helped to keep the salience of business and labor low because the rank and file people never really figured out what the committee was supposed to be doing.

> PRINCiple 7.7: Bureaucrats use jargon and committees
> for the political purpose of keeping salience low.

With the low-profile approach, LaStrange was able to get greater cooperation out of the mayor's office and at the same time help to highlight business and labor's differences over the uses of more productive housing technologies. Because they had no fears of being forced or

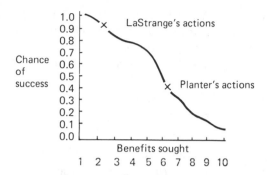

FIGURE 7-1. Relationship between probability of success and benefits sought in getting higher productivity in housing in the Los Angeles area.

bribed to do anything, labor and business never developed the coalition under LaStrange's strategy that they would have under Planter's. At this point, the intrusion of new information via the film presented by the vice-president of Kwiki Homes, Inc. had a maximum effect. It helped to change the attitudes of the two most powerful groups—business and labor—so they were willing to sponsor a moderate proposal for the adoption of new techniques. Once the representative from the mayor's office saw this happening, he cooperated by helping to change some of the building codes in the Los Angeles area.

It is clear that Planter ignored or did not understand the PRINCE method of solving political problems, and it is equally clear that LaStrange did. The final question that must be raised is whether or not we think LaStrange could have achieved any more than he did. If politics is the art of the possible, it is the responsibility of those using the PRINCE system to achieve the maximum, given the limits of feasibility. Did LaStrange settle for too little?

The problem can be illustrated by looking at the position of Planter and LaStrange on the graph appearing in Figure 7-1. That graph shows in the particular example we have used how the chances of success are related to the benefits sought. Notice that the more you seek, the smaller are your chances of success. It is completely analogous to horse racing, where you may bet on long odds and have a small chance of winning a lot of money, or bet on short odds and have a good chance of winning a small amount.* The two "x's" in Figure 7-1 mark the level of benefits sought and the chances of success for LaStrange and Planter. The former played it safe while the latter shot for the moon and achieved no results. The question is whether or not LaStrange could have shot

---

*This is not to imply that the PRINCE system has yet been completely adapted for use in betting on horse races.

for more benefits (represented on a 1–10 scale) without appreciably lowering his chances of getting some success. The way the curve is drawn suggests that he could have. It flattens out between benefits of 2 and 5, which means that the chances of success don't drop very much. Conversely, if Planter had shot for a 5 instead of an 8, he would have increased his chances of success 100 percent.

> PRINCiple 7.8: One must always match the chances of success of various alternatives with the relative benefits that would result from the success.

Even so, we should not be too critical of LaStrange. It is even more difficult to draw correctly a line for this kind of graph than it is to fill out the PRINCE charts. There are ways of translating the numbers in the PRINCE accounting system to the graph represented in Figure 7-1, but that involves a course called "The Advance Dynamics of the PRINCE Accounting System and Related Ideas in Political Problem Solving." Very few people have received this kind of training and LaStrange was not one of them. We must understand and even excuse his failure to use this graph. When compared to Planter, LaStrange wins hands down.

Nevertheless, there is a tendency for bureaucrats to pick benefits that do not take advantage of the proper mixture of maximum gain with minimum chance of failure. Generally speaking, we advise that the actor choose benefits when no less than a .5 chance of success is indicated. A .500 batting average in politics would be as spectacular as a .500 batting average in the American League. Bureaucrats tend to pick goals for which there is greater than .8 chance of succeeding. This is why most people think they are losers—their victories are almost always insignificant. Our advice based on the PRINCE system is that bureaucrats should continue to avoid the self-destructive impulses of a Bobby Planter but try to be a little bit more daring than a Mortimer LaStrange. To do this adequately, however, they will have to enroll in the advance course mentioned above.

Traffic Lights and Property Taxes: The Tale of Two Princes

8

We have frequently claimed that the PRINCE system is a useful device for seeking all sorts of pleasantries in life—both broad public goals, which everyone would agree are the result of political struggle, and the more private, personal gains, which we claim require action that is equally political. Up to now we have presented examples of primarily the broader, more public style of political seeking for rewards. As PRINCE players, George Washington, Ralph Nader, the princes from OWEC, and the protagonists in the Department of Housing were all struggling with questions whose outcome affected many members of the public.

But we remain firm in our belief that our definition of politics—getting people to act the way you want them to (when they don't want to) —is still fundamentally applicable to many problems of everyday life. In the beginning of the book we showed the applicability of the PRINCE charts to such intimate situations as a family decision-making session. In this chapter we will relate the tale of two different men attempting to wrangle with the government to get a favor that they badly want—and to which they quite honestly believe they are entitled.

Our first hero is Raymond Wilson, a thirty-five-year-old black man who lives in the central ghetto of Mega City, on the Eastern Seaboard. He lives in a deteriorating small house with his wife and four children, whose ages range from three to ten. Our second hero is Terry Ryan, Jr., a thirty-one-year-old dentist living in a $35,000 house far from the deteriorating center of Mega City, a home into which he recently moved after cramped city apartment living became intolerable.

87

To begin with, from a strictly formal point of view, both Wilson and Ryan (sorry, *Dr.* Ryan) live within the legal jurisdiction of Mega City. Ryan's house is suburban in its style and surrounding greenery, but it is legally within the city limits. Therefore they both vote in the same elections for mayor and congressman. (Needless to say, they don't always vote for the same candidate!) And as the vagaries of the mysterious art of election map drawing would have it, they both dwell in the same city council district. Their particular councilman views his district as a mushroom, a fact that greatly pleases him, although not because of any affinity for fungi. What makes the councilman so happy about this image is that this particular plant's thin stem arises out of a dark and festering spot, the central black ghetto, and stretches out to the boundaries of the city, the white peripheral neighborhoods, where its cap spreads to full width. Within the narrow stem live a few thousand voters whose skin is primarily the black color one would expect to find on the underside of a mushroom; within the broad cap live the several thousand voters who regularly return the incumbent to office; their dominant color is as white as would be expected in the upper regions of the plant. The incumbent feeds much more lustily off the political sustenance in the white cap than he does off the black-colored nether regions. These habits of the councilman are, we shall see, not without some significance for Wilson and Ryan.

Although they share some voting districts, Wilson and Ryan are not faced with identical political conditions. They have been blessed with different representatives in the state legislature and the two men and their respective sets of friends use different means to learn of the daily affairs around them. Wilson and his center city neighbors read the Mega City *Post-Autocrat*, a daily paper inclined to fulsome praise of Mega City, but otherwise of inconsistent political bias in its editorials and news reporting. Ryan and many of his neighbors also read the *Post-Autocrat*. But there is actually more thorough and fervent attention to the news reported in the weekly *Brighton Just-Eagle*, which takes its name from the area of the city it covers. The *Just-Eagle* loftily soars above such mundane news as foreign and domestic warfare and the interminable machinations in the nation's capital. Rather, its powerful talons grasp and lay bare the doings of the various local Leagues: Little, for the children; Junior, for the mommas; and Golfing, for the papas. Its unerring eye also never fails to spot the local significance of such city issues as zoning laws and the busing of children, topics that might serve, in the *Just-Eagle*'s phrase, "to upset the proper cultural mix of the Brighton neighborhood."

Newspaper circulation territories have no legal significance, of course, but much of the politics is the exchange of information. And in that respect—the information dimension of the political system—Wilson and Ryan inhabit quite different worlds.

In short, the two men operate in political systems that partly overlap. They share the same city government representatives but have different state legislators and sources of information. With that background firmly in mind, let's examine how Wilson and Ryan might go about using the PRINCE system in solving their political problems.

First consider Wilson, just home from work, sitting down to eat. It happens to be morning; Wilson is a night watchman and he eats dinner while his family eats breakfast. The table conversation is intense this morning; the topic even delays his wife's departure for her sales clerk's job in a downtown department store. The same topic has dominated their conversation for two days now, ever since their six-year-old son narrowly missed being hit by a car at a nearby corner on his way to school. By itself the incident was bad enough; what made it even worse was the fact that Wilson's nephew had been killed six months before at the same intersection. They were determined, although they didn't know how, to get a traffic light installed at that corner before someone else got killed.

At about the same time Ryan was discussing with his wife the cause of his rising political activism. The night before he had attended an open meeting sponsored by the city tax assessor for the Brighton neighborhood. The most notable thing Ryan remembered from the meeting—as if he could forget!—was what seemed to him a glaring inequity in the way the value of houses was assessed for tax purposes. It was the practice of the tax office to base the property tax of a house on its most recent purchase price. What this meant was that Ryan and others paid much higher taxes than did owners of homes that had not exchanged hands for many years (when house prices were much lower). From the figures made available, Ryan could see that some long-time owners (some of his older neighbors whose homes were clearly as valuable as his) were paying as much as $800 less in taxes per year. Ryan's tax bill of $1,200 per year hadn't seemed so bothersome before that meeting; the city provided better services than average in his area of the town and the local school was by all testimony one of the best in the city district. But to find that he was being asked to pay more than others in the same situation was intolerable. He resolved to get his tax assessment lowered.

Before looking at the strategies available to our two heroes, we must note that some people may argue that it is impossible to make meaningful comparisons between these two situations. No doubt many will assume that because Ryan is white and rich he is assured of success and because Wilson is black and poor he is assured of failure. But whoever makes such assumptions, and whether they are made out of jealousy or guilt, is likely to be wrong in at least one respect. Ryan admittedly has important advantages over Wilson. (There is also no denying the fact that the reasons for Ryan's advantage are matters of great concern in American society today. However, these concerns are not the subject to be dealt with here. Even so powerful a tool as the PRINCE system cannot alleviate all of society's injustices and inequalities.) Despite their dissimilar positions in society, Ryan and Wilson have two features in common as they start their quest for private help from the government: (1) neither has much chance of success and (2) each can better his chances by using the PRINCE calculations. But to remind ourselves of the political facts of life, the shrewdest calculations by either man using the PRINCE system can do no more than improve the unfavorable odds of something like one chance of success in ten to something like one chance in nine.

However different the goals and relative advantages of the two men, we shall see as we begin to hypothesize on the strategies they might use, the truth in the old adage that "all men are equal in the sight of PRINCE." Both men, to wring full advantage out of their rather bleak situations, must follow many of the same procedures in using the PRINCE system. In the discussion to follow, we shall show how comparable their calculations are. To simplify the presentation of the comparison between Wilson and Ryan, we shall deal only with each one's primary issue of concern—for Wilson, getting a street light; for Ryan, getting a lower tax assessment. A complete PRINCE strategy plan would require each man to include other issues of importance to the actors in the system he must deal with. But our present discussion is, if you will accept the phrase, academic comparison rather than a specific guide to action.

For both Wilson and Ryan there is little doubt where to start in formally setting down the system. Both men are necessarily concerned with getting favorable response from a single government official, a key decision maker whose cooperation is necessary for the success of either man. For Wilson this key decision maker is Mega City's commissioner of transportation; for Ryan this key official is the city tax assessor. If either of our heroes could go and reason with the appropriate official, this would be the end of the problem—one way or another. In most cases the direct approach is unlikely to work, even to the extent of getting personal access to the key decision maker. However, it might nevertheless be worth trying. First, it might just succeed, in spite of its low probability. Second, trying this direct approach will demonstrate to anyone who cares that an applicant has tried to be direct and honest. (A reputation for directness and honesty is far from a handicap in politics.) Finally, and at the very least, even a thwarted attempt to appeal directly to the key decision maker should provide some valuable information about the person and the system to be manipulated.

PRINCiple 8.1: Exhaust all routine options before executing a political strategy.

We shall assume that both men are forced to go beyond the key decision maker. They must, therefore, compile a longer list of relevant actors. The prime criterion for including any more actors (in both cases) is to find those actors who can put the right pressure on the key decision maker. As you might imagine, picking out such people is no easy matter. The PRINCE system does not indicate how to gather political intelligence in specifics. It does provide the general framework that points to the types of intelligence that should be gathered.

In our story of Wilson and Ryan, we shall assume that they have identified six actors besides the key decision maker whom they will consider in their political system. The same six categories appear to be important to both men. In some of the categories, as we shall see, the same individual will play quite different roles in Wilson's and Ryan's political systems.

PRINCiple 8.2: Look for actors in the following general categories: governmental officials, party supporters, extracommunity actors, the legal system, and the mass media.

Governmental Influencer

The first place to look for someone who influences a governmental official is another official. In this case the most proximate governmental influencer for Wilson's and Ryan's key decision maker is the previously mentioned city councilman who unbiasedly serves all groups in his constituency without respect to race, creed, or religion—merely caring about the number of votes they can muster. We shall see below that this same individual is a different actor because of his differing relationship to Wilson and Ryan; and he is also a different actor from the standpoint of his relationship to the key decision maker.

Party Influencer

Whenever we find competitive electoral politics, we also find party or other political leaders who may not hold any formal office, but who wield tremendous influence because of their ability to help officials get elected and re-elected. For both our PRINCE players the primary party influencer is a member of the Democratic party, but their similarities scarcely go beyond this label. Wilson's neighborhood is the domain of one of the leading political figures in the city, a man whose full-time job (and, some say, his several full-time salaries) is based upon his continuing work for the health and growth of the Democratic party in the city.

PRINCiple 8.3:   Bureaucrats have little power over broad public policy questions; but they often have tremendous power vis-à-vis limited decisions that can be very important to individuals. Therefore, don't ignore them in your calculations.

Ryan's chief political contact is Winston Smith III, a patrician Democrat whose time is much more occupied with his management of the Brighton Real Estate Corporation than with party matters, which he considers more of a hobby and marginal investment in self-advertisement.

Extracommunity Influencer

The American political system frequently contains multiple opportunities for appealing an unfavorable decision; most of these channels are informal. For example, legislators in the state and national capital will occasionally respond to appeals from local constituents even though they have no formal jurisdiction over the issue at hand.

Wilson and Ryan share the same congressman; although this individual, too, would act differently toward the two men. However, the PRINCE system would advise both men not to make the same mistake so many citizens do: namely, trying to get their congressman in Washington to straighten out a local matter at home. It is generally a good idea to write your congressmen about national matters but not about your own private political problems. Except for rare circumstances, most congressmen in the United States have very low power on local private issues.

Wilson and Ryan's congressman would not be a very useful extracommunity influencer, but their respective state assemblymen might be. Wilson is represented—at least he is supposed to be—in the state legislature by a protégé of the political boss. This state assemblyman is elected from a district shaped something like the councilman's. His most sizable voting constituency is Italian, and by one of those strange but frequent coincidences of American politics he himself is of Italian parentage. Ryan's delegate to the state assembly is a legislative veteran whose chief identifiable contribution to the body politic was his sound judgment in marrying the eldest sister of Winston Smith III some twenty years earlier. He has generally rested on her laurels since that time.

Legal Influencer

It used to be said that lawyers were ambulance-chasers because of their affinity for turning a personal injury into a legal claim. This name is no longer valid in every case. A few lawyers are too busy creating legal issues out of the plight of civil rights leaders, professional athletes, long-haired high school students, and countless others to be able to concentrate solely on ambulances. Occasionally, the ambulances have been left to chase themselves. Wilson or Ryan may find it expedient to pay the costs in money, time, and effort to have a lawyer convert their personal grievance into a legal claim that may be settled in court.

Mass Media Influencer

We spoke earlier of the two newspapers by which Wilson and Ryan learn of the political world surrounding them. The newspapers can, of course, serve the political actor as much more than a source of information. The press may be used to stir up fevered attention to some cause, attention so fevered and widespread that the most aloof government official will have to take notice. Public opinion is difficult to arouse, and once aroused can be very unruly—even to the extent of turning on its arouser. It nevertheless may be viewed as an actor to be used by Wilson or Ryan.

We can summarize the political standing of our two pursuers of special interest by referring to the PRINCE charts, in somewhat modified form. We shall deal here with only the one issue of prime concern to each man. And we shall present the issue position, salience, and power of each general actor for Wilson and Ryan.

Both men face the same problem: the only actor in the system with any salience also has extensive power and a negative attitude on the issue. The reason the key decision maker has salience and power is that the community has given him the authority to make decisions in the area. The reason he has a negative position is that he gets pleas for favors every day of the week; he adopts a general negative attitude so as to discourage anything that will create additional paperwork for him. His

CHART 8-1. Issue position, power, and salience in Wilson's and Ryan's political systems.

Actor	Wilson Position	Wilson power	Wilson Salience	Ryan Position	Ryan power	Ryan Salience
Key decision maker	−1	+3	+3	−1	+3	+3
Government influencer (City Councilman)	+1	+3	0	+1	+2	0
Party influencer	+3	+2	0	+3	+3	0
State Assemblyman	+3	+1	0	+3	+3	0
Local court	+1	+2	0	+1	+3	0
Mass media	+2	+2	0	+1	+2	0

issue position could be altered if the other actors in the system bring pressure on him. However, none of them attach any importance to the issue. Consequently there is no inclination on their part to generate such pressure.

The strategic imperative for both Wilson and Ryan is quite clear from Chart 8-1. Each must raise the salience of those political actors who have power and who have the capacity to change the decision maker's issue position. However, the similarity stops at this point because the power of the other actors is very different to our two citizen-politicians. For Wilson, the power is so spread out that he must get three or four actors to have high salience. In contrast, Ryan need only get the political leader of Brighton or almost any combination of two other actors.

> PRINCiple 8.4: The degree to which power is centralized or decentralized among the political actors should shape your political strategies.

Another basic difference in the political situation for Wilson and Ryan is illustrated by the friendship-neutrality-hostility patterns among the political actors. As Charts 8-2 and 8-3 indicate, there is less overall political friendship among the actors in Wilson's political system than there is in Ryan's. We have discovered this fact by looking at the ratio of minuses to pluses in the friendship-neutrality-hostility charts. For Wilson the ratio is fifteen minuses to eleven pluses while Ryan's chart has a ratio of six minuses to twenty-three pluses. The procedure of checking for the degree of total friendship-neutrality-hostility is usually recommended at the outset for all PRINCE political planning. In this particular case, it shows that Wilson is dealing with a much more fragmented and hostile overall political environment than is Ryan.

CHART 8-2. Friendship-neutrality-hostility patterns
for Wilson's political system.

This actor	Key decision maker	Govern- ment influencer	Party influ- encer	State Assembly- man	Local court	Mass media
			Feels about this actor			
Key decision maker	X	–	+	–	–	–
Government influencer	–	X	+	–	–	+
Party influencer	+	+	X	+	–	–
State Assemblyman	0	+	+	X	–	+
Local court	–	–	–	0	X	+
Mass media	0	–	–	+	0	X

PRINCiple 8.5: The patterns of friendship-neutrality-
hostility among the political actors should shape
your political strategies.

We have assumed that Wilson and Ryan try, without success, to talk
directly with the official in charge. Their next step is to decide how to
approach the other actors in the system. Remembering the differences
in power and friendship-neutrality-hostility patterns, let's look at the
strategies the two might follow.

PRINCiple 8.6:   Use friendship-neutrality-hostility charts
to decide who should exert influence to change
issue positions.

In approaching the councilman (the chief government influencer on
the key decision maker), the two will be faced with radically different
situations, although they will be talking to the same man. Wilson is
black and poor and represents only a tiny minority of the councilman's
district. He will be lucky if he can talk to anyone but an assistant to the
councilman's assistant. Whomever he does see will tell him that he
should check with the Department of Transportation about his request.
When Wilson replies that he already has, without success, the councilman's assistant will offer a firm promise to "see what I can do."
    Ryan, by contrast, comes from the wealthy and numerous majority
in the councilman's district. He will have no trouble seeing the councilman himself, who will assure him that he will do everything in his

CHART 8-3. Friendship-neutrality-hostility patterns
for Ryan's political system.

| | Feels about this actor | | | | | |
This actor	Key decision maker	Govern- ment influencer	Party influ- encer	State Assembly- man	Local court	Mass media
Key decision maker	X	+	+	+	+	–
Government influencer	+	X	+	+	–	+
Party influencer	+	+	X	+	+	–
State Assemblyman	+	+	+	X	+	+
Local court	+	–	+	0	X	–
Mass media	–	+	+	+	+	X

power to make sure that the tax assessor reconsiders his problem. However, despite Ryan's better treatment, he is actually little better off
than Wilson. Ryan's most substantial gain is only a slightly less vague
promise of help than Wilson received. And in Mega City the administration of the Tax Department is more insulated from council pressure
than the Transportation Department. So the councilman has less power
to influence Ryan's key decision maker than he does Wilson's. In Wilson's case, the council does have the power to overrule the Department
of Transportation. In Ryan's case, the council does not have this power.
So the outcome is negative for both men.

In fact, a rational calculation of time and probable results would dic-
tate not even trying to get help from the councilman. But for both men
the prospects of any one course of action are so slim that to have any
hope of success every stone must be turned. In Ryan's case the effort
may have beneficial side effects because the councilman does have
friendly relations with the tax assessor and other important actors;
these may serve to provide Ryan access to other contact points.

The next actor, the party influencer, or the political boss, constitutes
an important alternative for both Wilson and Ryan. In Wilson's case,
the political boss is the major figure in Mega City's Democratic party.
Because the party controls the city government, he has considerable
power. Unfortunately, this boss is not like the ones who used to run
cities fifty years ago. These men would build their power upon frequent
small favors for the lower and middle classes. The boss in Mega City today derives his power from his ability to raise money for the party. Consequently he has never even seen the street corner with which Wilson is
concerned. This particular boss has strong political friendships with
many of the actors, so Wilson has to try (but there is little chance that
he will succeed) to raise the boss's salience for Wilson's issue.

Ryan stands a much better chance of enlisting his political boss's support. As owner of the largest real estate firm in the Brighton neighborhood, Winston Smith has an interest in keeping residents satisfied with the tax situation, and for that matter, with everything that affects the area. Moreover, Smith has strong friendly ties with all of the important political actors and has sufficient power to counteract the tax assessor's position. However, receiving a sympathetic ear and changing his salience sufficiently to help Ryan are two different things. Unless there is some special reason (such as Ryan's superb job on Winston Smith IV's rotten teeth or pressure from other friendly actors), there is only a limited chance that he will help Ryan by telling the assessor to lower the rate.

Both Wilson and Ryan would probably be better off seeing the state assemblymen. In fact, Ryan's assemblyman has married into the family of Winston Smith III. Wilson's assemblyman has sufficient friendly ties to be of use, and perhaps would want to court the black vote. Unfortunately, his power is still rather slight.

If approaching the local and state politicians fails, Wilson and Ryan might find the local courts helpful. The charts indicate that the local courts have substantial power in both areas, although they are more likely to exercise power in tax matters than on the question of traffic lights. If the local courts can be enlisted, they will raise their issue position to +3 and their salience to +3, which will probably be sufficient to overcome the resistance of the key decision maker. There are of course some problems associated with going to the courts.

The first problem is cost. Neither Wilson nor Ryan could find a lawyer who would take the time necessary to construct a case without a substantial fee. Lawyers sell their time. Unless they can make money on a case, they hesitate to take it. Getting a traffic light put up or changing a tax assessment is not nearly so profitable as a $50,000 whiplash case. For these reasons, Ryan would probably get a cheaper price than Wilson because a lawyer would see Ryan (but not Wilson) as a potential client in the future. A juicy malpractice suit or divorce could be the product of the lawyer's efforts in Ryan's case. But association with Wilson could lead to nothing in the future but more unprofitable public issue work.

Another problem with the courts is that there must exist something approximating a legal wrong before a court will interfere. Some legal symbol must be invoked to prove the illegality of a failure to install a traffic light or to lower Ryan's assessment. We shouldn't overemphasize the difficulties here, because it is the job of the lawyer to envelop the desires of his clients in the symbolic garb of legal rights and duties and it is the job of the judge to pretend that he is applying legal rules in making his decisions.

In the cases of both Wilson and Ryan, the obvious plea is that these individuals are being deprived of their equal rights. Wilson is being treated unequally because he lives in conditions that warrant a stoplight at his corner and because others living under the same conditions have such stoplights (especially in the Italian neighborhood). Ryan is being treated unequally because those who have lived longer in the Brighton area have lower taxes even though they might have more expensive houses. Assuming they can get a lawyer and can afford what he wants for his work, both Wilson and Ryan stand a reasonable chance of success through the courts.

Finally, we come to the last actor on our list—public opinion. This actor should be viewed as a tool that Wilson or Ryan might be able to use not only to influence the Department of Transportation or the tax assessor but also to influence each of the other actors. Public opinion is like an untrained dinosaur. If Wilson or Ryan can do what is necessary to arouse public opinion, it will scare the apathy out of all the other actors, although it might turn around and devour Wilson or Ryan. In short, to use public opinion Wilson and Ryan will have to invest a great deal of time and may ultimately create a situation in which the chances of success are lower than they were before the public got involved in the first place.

The reason the appeal to public opinion can be so effective is that public opinion can hit the other actors where it hurts. The head of the traffic division or the tax assessor can get fired if the councilman or whoever controls his job sees the need for a handy scapegoat. The councilman and assemblymen can lose votes in the next election or—worse—generate a split within their party machine by providing some up-and-coming politico a cause to become well known to the public. The political boss who seems relatively invulnerable to the consequence of a bad press is usually sensitive to the public at least to the extent of withdrawing support from the existing incumbents. Finally, even the courts and the lawyers who feed off the courts find the awareness of a public issue to be stimulating. It isn't necessary to be a naïve believer in democracy to keep in mind that the public, especially as it is represented through the mass media, can raise salience, change issue positions, and even alter power relationships.

The problem, as we have already said, is that the costs are extremely high and the consequences hard to predict and control once events establish their own momentum. For this reason, the public should be approached only after other avenues have been explored. This advice is especially true for Ryan who, as the PRINCE figures show, has some reasonsble chance working through more private stratagems. In fact, given the closed nature of the Brighton political system, if Ryan can't succeed by approaching the political actors we have already discussed, there is a good chance arousing the public will not result in anything but a decline in his profits from his dental business.

However, Ryan might nevertheless find his ego sufficiently hurt to go to the public. If he does, we have a few tips to pass on to him. In an issue such as tax assessment, there is the problem of relative cost and benefit to those in the public. Those who have been living in Brighton for a long period of time will be opposed to Ryan's position because their self-interest will be threatened. Self-interest does not always guide the public reaction, but in an issue that is so complicated and so clearly connected to economic interests, it will be critical. Hence, only those in a similar disadvantaged position will find the issue appealing.

A rough calculation of the ratio of newcomers to permanent old residents should be made to see whether or not the public awareness of the issue will help or hinder Ryan. Unless there is a substantial percentage of newcomers in Ryan's position with the tax assessor, he might as well forget the public. Even with favorable conditions Ryan still will have to fight those who control the area newspaper to get proper publicity for the issue. The best that Ryan would be able to do is to get some local figure to state publicly that the existing procedure is unfair; and given the importance of reputation, he may be able to swing a substantial number of individuals.

In short, Ryan has only a slim chance if he goes to the public. To build a political organization around one issue like tax assessment is practically impossible. To get the public in the town to express the feeling that Ryan has been the subject of serious injustice is highly unlikely. To have sympathetic reporting from a newspaper (which, among other things, is indebted to Winston Smith III) is beyond reasonable expectation. Ryan's only chance of creating sufficient public pressure would be to build up a community of friends over several years to support his issue. Unfortunately (or fortunately) by that time, his tax assessment will be lower than those in newer houses, and he will no doubt be leading the opposing forces.

For Wilson, the role of the public is a different prospect if only because he has little hope through the other actors. The issue itself has more general public appeal because it involves what is normally considered to be a relatively simple matter—the protection of a child's life. Of course, if the bureaucrats get hold of the issue with a discussion of per capita traffic lights and the kilowatt hours per decade needed to support the light, the simple issue may get drowned in detail. However, with a little bit of luck and some help from the news media, the questions of costs and benefits will never be raised.

Moreover, Wilson occupies a neighborhood in which hundreds of people are affected directly by the traffic light. He has a wide range of natural allies that he can mobilize to write letters, make telephone calls, and, if publicity is required, to stage protests. The group should not get too vocal or its actions will be treated in the media as a riot and evidence of racial tension. Well-modulated demonstrations, even by blacks, can succeed in getting press and media coverage so that some politician will attempt to reap the glory by bringing pressure to bear on the right people.

If Wilson is unable to get a sufficient public response by calling for changes to protect the life of his child and others, he might embark upon a potentially potent but more dangerous strategy. He could wrap the issue in the symbol of racism by pointing out that similar situations in the Italian neighborhoods do not exist. The trouble with this strategy is that it awakens the Italians to the fact that the appeal for a traffic light in Wilson's block may cost them another traffic light in their block. It might also serve to allow politicians to say Wilson has polarized the community—a term used by politicians to ignore the initial issue by raising the specter of revolution. But it may also light the torch of public relations that attracts the attention of the news or television media and of politicians.

In any case, by going to the ultimate arbiter—the public—Mr. Wilson will have at least achieved the satisfaction of doing something. He will receive all types of ego satisfactions and will have convinced himself that he has tried. He will also probably have served notice to the politicians and bureaucrats to be more responsive to the public in such situations in the future. As in almost all political acts, the costs would not be equal to the benefits for Wilson, but from a long–term perspective it may be worthwhile to the community at large.

Before ending this chapter, it might be useful to return to the question of who has more power—the black ghetto-dweller or the white suburbanite. The answer should be relatively clear that in general neither has much power except in terms of their relative wealth. Instead, the charts indicate that the reason for the greater responsiveness to Ryan is the greater power enjoyed by the political actors in his political system and the general friendliness and cooperation existing among the political actors. Wilson can't find those who have power because the power enjoyed by any one actor in his political world is relatively small. Also, the lack of good working relationships among the various political actors creates problems for Wilson that Ryan does not have.

The system is not all stacked in Ryan's favor, however. If he can't get the major actors to make the changes for him, there is little he can do. The high friendship among the actors makes the system work in such a way that there is little to do once you have talked to the powerful people. Going to the public, as we have indicated, will probably yield negative results. In contrast, Wilson can continue to fight and can hope for success even after being turned down by the powers that be. He can use public opinion and can hope to find a crusader who will fight the existing bureaucracy.

In our discussion, we have left out some obvious factors that could be operating for both Wilson and Ryan. Racism throughout the city administration and the political system could prevent Wilson from even being heard by those with any power. Bribes and other forms of grease to make the system work might be the only road that Wilson can follow; if so, his lack of wealth would preclude his success. Similarly, Ryan could be faced by the ever-present conflict between the old and new residents or he could be living in a community in which the tax assessment is purely a function of how many bottles of liquor you buy for the assessor. These types of conditions alter the dynamics of the system and must be included in the PRINCE calculations.

Neal Bellos

Saving Middle City's Neighborhood Health Center: A PRINCE Replay

9

At one point in my career I served as the director for a local antipoverty program in Middle City. Such programs were established during the 1960s by the federal government in an effort to improve the health, education, and welfare of the poor in America. Many of these human service programs required political manipulation not only between the federal government and local communities but also among members of the local communities. Let me tell you of an experience that caused me to apply many of the basic principles of the PRINCE political accounting system to the establishment of a neighborhood health center in Middle City before the system was set forth on paper.

One day in the early winter of the mid-1960s I had a luncheon meeting with a good friend and colleague on the faculty of Middle City University and active in community politics. I always enjoyed these lunches because my colleague kept me posted on many of the current developments in Middle City. I used these lunches not only to share experiences but to gain advice and counsel from my colleague. At this particular lunch, he informed me that the Neighborhood Health Center proposal that was being discussed in the community was dead. When I inquired why it was dead, he informed me that the health facility proposal had engendered such opposition in Middle City that there seemed to be no possibility of this program being implemented. I was both upset and angered at my colleague's rather casual announcement because I had been given assurances that federal funds had been allocated to Middle City for the purpose of instituting a neighborhood health facility. I also knew the release of these funds for this important project was depen-

103

dent only upon the receipt of a suitable proposal that met the Office of Economic Opportunity guidelines. The thought that some local opposition would deprive our community of this valuable program really angered me. When my anger cooled, I decided the situation called for careful planning to select an appropriate action.

My first step was to make a very careful assessment of the present situation by tracing the steps that led to the present problem. Toward this end I called together my associate director for program planning and the mayor's executive assistant for federal affairs. These individuals had been involved with the planning process to establish the Neighborhood Health Center and both had a great deal of contact with individuals working on it. Based on our discussion of the available information, I'd like to tell you how I handled the situation using the terminology of the PRINCE political accounting system. (Obviously, I didn't use the PRINCE terminology at that time. The Neighborhood Health Center issue occurred several years before the PRINCE method was developed. However, my planning and subsequent actions were so consistent with PRINCE that the use of its terminology makes for an insightful example of practical application.)

Getting the PRINCE Picture

My first task was to define the issue—the establishment of a Neighborhood Health Center in Middle City. My second step was to identify the individual actors engaged in the issue.

The first major actor was Dr. Goodguy. In the summer of that year Dr. Goodguy, a young physician who had just completed a tour of duty in the Public Health Service in the state, came to Middle City with the idea of establishing a neighborhood health facility to serve the poor in our community. Dr. Goodguy had several outstanding characteristics. First, he was an extremely knowledgeable physician and was very much aware of the health needs of both rural and urban poor people. Second, he was very much committed to the liberal social issues of the time and had a special commitment to improving the lot of this nation's poor. Third, he had very close friendships with key decision makers in the Office of Economic Opportunity, particularly those who were engaged in implementing neighborhood health facilities to serve the poor. When he arrived in Middle City, Dr. Goodguy had virtual assurance that if he could generate interest in this idea, funding for the health facility would be forthcoming. In addition he had a wide variety of social connections in Middle City, including some of the more liberal and progressive community leaders. These connections gave him access to certain interests active in promoting or initiating community service activities.

One of the initial stops Dr. Goodguy made upon his arrival in the community was at my office. He shared with me his idea of working to establish this Neighborhood Health Center, indicating he had a certain community following that was very interested in working out the necessary arrangements. I heartily encouraged his activities, believing that it would be an excellent idea if he and a group of citizens could develop their proposal by themselves. I suggested that he submit the written proposal to the Community Action Agency, which could endorse it for funding by OEO. This course of action was appealing because it seemed to me it would be a way of demonstrating the maximum feasible participation clause of the Economic Opportunity Act of 1964. Most local antipoverty programs at that time had been established by federal directive or under the control of the local Community Action Agency with minimal citizen initiative and involvement. Therefore, I believed that with Dr. Goodguy on the scene, our community had an excellent opportunity not only to get a valued Neighborhood Health Center, but also to demonstrate independent and self-initiating citizen action.

The next actor involved in the Neighborhood Health Center was an individual I'll refer to as Dr. Esteem. Dr. Esteem is an eminent physician in the community who is also very committed to progressive social action. He is highly respected by his colleagues in the medical community and became closely associated with Dr. Goodguy in the planning of the Neighborhood Health Center.

The third actor was a group that Dr. Goodguy worked with during the planning phases of the Neighborhood Health Center: the Citizens' Committee for Human Development (CCHD) in Middle City. This is a long-active committee composed of the liberal element of middle and upper-middle class citizens who are interested in structuring opportunities for social progress in the community. This group is generally found at the hub of progressive movements to improve health, education, community relations, and antipoverty services. The CCHD is quite a vocal group operating independent of the local political process. They are not held in very high esteem by the local elected government officials; to say that the relationship of the CCHD to local public officials is antagonistic might be an understatement. Members of the CCHD are often the most outspoken critics of the local government's activities. They have little disposition to curb their criticism, which often makes headlines in the local newspapers. For purposes of identifying an individual actor for the PRINCE chart, I have selected the CCHD chairperson, who was an active participant in the planning process along with Dr. Goodguy and Dr. Esteem.

The other major actors in this particular issue were determined not so much by local preference as by OEO guidelines for planning neighborhood health facilities. Most neighborhood health facilities were traditionally established under the auspices of some health or medical organization or institution (e.g., a medical school or public health department). For any proposal to be successfully funded through Washington, the local community had to indicate that all the medical and health interests were in accord and would play a role in establishing and operating these neighborhood health facilities. So in this regard the major actors in Middle City were (1) the chairperson of the County Medical Society (It is very important to know that at this time Middle City was somewhat backward and conservative in certain areas of community relations. The community had not yet succeeded in achieving full racial integration or even desegregation of many of its facilities. Thus the County Medical Society was composed of white doctors.), (2) the chairperson of the Black Medical Society, (3) the Dean of the Medical School, and (4) the director of the City-County Public Health Department.

With the major actors on the health proposal identified, we can now estimate issue positions. The following information for filling out the issue positions was developed out of my discussion with the associate director for planning and the mayor's executive assistant. We discussed Dr. Goodguy's issue position and concluded it was reasonable to give him a +3 on this particular issue. Dr. Esteem was rated as a +2. He very much favored the issue, but not as much as Dr. Goodguy. We also decided to give the chairperson of the Citizens' Committee for Human Development a +3 in accord with the general disposition of this group when they seized upon current popular progressive issues. They always had a high degree of support for issues that were both socially and politically attractive to them. When it came to an assessment of the issue position of the other major actors, the executive assistant to the mayor was helpful. In his work and social relations he had direct contact with all the other major actors, and they had informed him of their reactions to Dr. Goodguy's plans. On this particular issue, we put down a –1 for the chairperson of the County Medical Society. The chairperson at this time was an eminent physician whose family had been among the original settlers of Middle City. He and his family had always occupied leadership positions in Middle City affairs. Despite his history of community leadership, particularly in the improvement of medical care, we rated him as –1 on this issue. After all, as chairperson of the County Medical Society, he was still committed to the notion of health care by fee for service, and the Neighborhood Health Center bordered on socialized medicine. The chairperson of the Black Medical Society in Middle City was in a very interesting position. As we assessed that particular group, there were two factions. One faction was the younger physicians who were very much in favor of the idea of a neighborhood health facility to meet the needs of the poor. At the same time, the older black physicians were somewhat against the notion of the Neighborhood Health Center. The proposed location for the Neighborhood Health Center was in the neighborhood where most of the older physicians practiced medicine. It was reasonable to believe that the establishment of the Neighborhood Health Center would act as a direct conflict to their self-interest. Our assessment of the Black Medical Society was a –1 on this particular issue, a very close and split decision. The Dean of the Medical School, we decided, was a –2. Although the leadership of the Medical School stood for progress in the delivery of health care services, the Dean is the sort of person who is against any idea he did not originate. The director of the City-County Public Health Department was given a –1 on the issue of the Neighborhood Health Center because he generally took a position in line with his health colleagues.

The total of the issue positions is +3, giving some indication at first blush that the issue has certain support in the community and may pass (see Chart 9-1). As we all well know, the usual means of assessing the outcome of a group decision is based on the simple accounting of the pros and cons on the particular issue. Therefore, after the initial discussions between Dr. Goodguy and his supporters, it appeared that the Neighborhood Health Center had some credence in Middle City. However, this initial conclusion was made without the benefit of the other penetrating insights provided by the PRINCE analysis.

CHART 9-1. Issue: Establishment of Neighborhood Health Center.

Actors	Issue position		Power		Product of issue position times power		Salience		Total support by actor
Dr. Goodguy	+3	X	1	=	+3	X	3	=	+9
Dr. Esteem	+2	X	2	=	+4	X	1	=	+4
Chairperson CCHD	+3	X	1	=	+3	X	3	=	+9
County Medical Society Chairperson	–1	X	3	=	–3	X	2	=	–6
Black Medical Society Chairperson	–1	X	3	=	–3	X	2	=	–6
Dean of Medical School	–2	X	3	=	–6	X	3	=	–18
Director City-County Public Health Department	–1	X	2	=	–2	X	2	=	–4
Total	+3				–4				–12

We then turned our attention to an assessment of the individual actor's power to affect the outcome of this decision. We assessed Dr. Goodguy's power and gave him a value of 1. We were not being less than charitable in assigning such a low figure to him; Middle City, as I mentioned before, is a rather conservative community and outsiders are viewed unfavorably. There are people who have lived in Middle City for nearly twenty years and are still not considered permanent members of the community. Therefore, one can easily imagine how the landed aristocracy will react when a young outsider arrives on the decision-making scene talking about free medical services based on funding from Washington. Dr. Esteem was given a value of 2 because he is a respected member of the health community. The power of the Citizens' Committee for Human Development was assessed at 1. Outspoken liberals had little impact on the major decision makers in the community at that time. The CCHD had been critical of every service institution and organization in the community. In addition, the CCHD took every public opportunity to vent criticism at most of the titular leadership in the community. In this case, as we assessed it that evening, CCHD's basic power was to lend moral support to Dr. Goodguy; but they would have minimal influence on local decision making. The major power to affect the outcome of this decision was actually vested in the members of the health community, specifically the physicians, because Washington funding guidelines placed the opinions of the medical fraternity in an important position. The proposal needed the support and contributions of all major community health interests; if any of these interests was against the health facility, OEO would probably not fund this project. Therefore each of the medical interests, the chairperson of the County Medical Society, the chairperson of the Black Medical Society, and the Dean of the Medical School, was given a power of 3. Because of the guidelines, each of these actors could virtually block the issue. Finally, we assigned a power of 2 to the director of the City-County Public Health Department. Once again, he was influential, but we ranked him below his other medical colleagues. Now, if we multiply each actor's power times issue position and add these seven products, we have a total of −4 (see Chart 9-1). The inclusion of the power factor changes an issue that was originally cast in a favorable light to an issue with a negative outcome.

The next information that we collected was salience. To Dr. Goodguy, who was intensely interested in this program, we gave a value of 3. Dr. Esteem, although in favor of this issue and with some degree of power to affect the outcome, had a salience of 1 on this particular issue. His salience certainly did not match that of Dr. Goodguy because he was engaged in several other projects at that time. The CCHD was also given a salience figure of 3. They had other projects going, but all were with a high degree of salience. The leaders in the medical field developed a fairly high degree of salience on this issue. The mayor's executive assistant informed us that the chairperson of the County Medical Society had a salience approaching that of 2. The chairperson was against the issue and had power to affect the outcome. He was beginning to feel badgered and bothered by an outsider telling the medical community what it should do. Therefore his salience rose because of the pressures being exerted by his contacts. The same was true with the Black Medical Society, whose members felt they were being lectured at and told how to serve their patients in the black community. The Dean of the Medical School was rather angered by Dr. Goodguy. The more they came into contact, the more a personality clash developed until, finally, the Dean would become livid whenever Dr. Goodguy appeared at any community forum. The director of the City-County Public Health Department, not to be outdone by his colleagues, was also slated with a salience of 2. Now if we complete the multiplication prescribed by the PRINCE chart, we arrive at the following figures for total support by each actor: Dr. Goodguy, +9; Dr. Esteem, +4; CCHD chairperson, +9; County Medical Society chairperson, -6; Black Medical Society chairperson, -6; Dean of the Medical School, -18; and director of the City-County Public Health Department, -4. All actors' total support is -12. This figure accounts for my colleague's luncheon report to me that the Neighborhood Health Center was dead. We tried to determine how we might intervene to reverse the outcome of this particular issue. In spite of the ready availability of federal funds to provide for a neighborhood health facility in Middle City, substantial local opposition on the part of very influential actors had been engendered. Unless something was changed, the issue would in fact be dead.

A Strategy Fit for a Prince

A look at the last column of Chart 9-1 makes it obvious that intervention has to take place with the medical leaders in order to reduce the impact of their negative numbers. Working with Dr. Goodguy and the Citizens' Committee for Human Development would not increase their positive numbers enough to overcome the opposition of the medical leadership.

A second strategy to gain more positive numbers in the last column is to add additional actors who might be favorably disposed to the establishment of a neighborhood health facility. With this strategy, the next step was the construction of the PRINCE analysis friendship-neutrality-hostility chart (Chart 9-2). Once again, the chart was not really calculated because the PRINCE system wasn't extant at that time. We did analyze the relationships between the actors in an attempt to determine with whom we might be able to work to effect a favorable outcome for the issue. A cursory glance at Chart 9-2 lends some insight to our reasoning. The first column shows how actors felt about Dr. Goodguy. Here we see that the medical fraternity is negatively disposed to the originator of the idea for a neighborhood health facility. As a matter of fact, because of the negative reaction toward Dr. Goodguy and his reciprocation toward the other actors, it was imperative that he maintain low profile in the next phases of intervention. As a matter of fact, I asked Dr. Goodguy as a personal favor not only to take a low profile but to absent himself from the community until we could resolve this issue one way or the other. Looking at Dr. Esteem's column it becomes apparent that the community is extremely favorably disposed toward him. Dr. Esteem emerged as an important actor in reversing the situation. With this insight I began to work closely with him and subsequently involved him in most of the contacts that I made after our analysis that evening. The analysis of the first PRINCE chart (Chart 9-1) with the negative outcome indicated that there would have to be direct intervention and interaction with the chairperson of the County Medical Society, the chairperson of the Black Medical Society, the Dean of the Medical School, and the director of the City-County Public Health

CHART 9-2. Friendship-neutrality-hostility chart.

This actor	Feels about this actor						Director City-County Public Health Department
	Dr. Goodguy	Dr. Esteem	CCHD Chairperson	County Medical Society Chairperson	Black Medical Society Chairperson	Dean of Medical School	
Dr. Goodguy	X	+	+	-	+	-	-
Dr. Esteem	+	X	+	+	+	-	-
CCHD Chairperson	+	+	X	-	+	-	-
County Medical Society Chairperson	-	+	-	X	0	+	+
Black Medical Society Chairperson	-	+	-	0	X	0	0
Dean of Medical School	-	+	-	+	0	X	0
Director City-County Public Health Department	-	+	-	+	0	+	X

Department regardless of the information from Chart 9-2. However, it is insightful to learn from the friendship-neutrality-hostility chart that the Dean of the Medical School was not well liked. There is also a general negative disposition toward the CCHD, indicating once again that this group would have to have somewhat of a low profile in the next phase of this project.

After filling out an analysis of the first two PRINCE charts, we made several decisions:

1. Intervention would have to take place with the prime actors representing the leadership in the medical community.
2. There would be some attempt to add new actors in the decision-making process with a disposition toward a favorable outcome.
3. Dr. Esteem emerged with a major interactive role. Dr. Goodguy and the chairperson of the Citizens' Committee for Human Development would have to maintain a low profile, staying out of the situation until it was resolved.

Armed with these fresh insights, we adjourned for that evening, and I had in my mind the strategies that next had to be pursued. The following morning I embarked on a new course of intervention in an attempt to rescue the idea of the Neighborhood Health Center for Middle City. The rest of my activities are described and illustrated by Chart 9-3.

The first task I faced was to describe the issue to be dealt with, but before I could do that I had a problem to analyze. The initial analysis of Charts 9-1 and 9-2 indicated that the medical leaders needed to have their total figures changed from extreme negatives toward positives. Being a person of eminent practicality with some notion of the limits of my own powers and realizing that the actor's positions were already fixed, I was not too sanguine about the possibility of changing the minds of those opposed to the neighborhood health facility. Before I proceeded to intervene, I needed some important information. I placed a call to the Washington, D.C., headquarters of Neighborhood Health Center Programs and asked them whether or not it was a prerequisite to have the active participation and concurrence of all the medical interests in the community before funding a neighborhood health facility. They said they did not require complete involvement and commitment of these medical interests but did require that no one in the medical community have any overt opposition to the Neighborhood Health Center. In other words, although most of the neighborhood health facilities were being established under health and medical auspices, this was not necessarily a requirement. Therefore, establishing a neighborhood health facility

CHART 9-3. Issue: Establishment of Neighborhood Health Center.

Actors	Issue position		Power	I × P		Salience		Total support by actor
Old Pro	+3	X	1	+3	X	3	=	+9
Dr. Esteem	+3	X	2	+6	X	2	=	+12
Chairperson Citizens' Committee for Human Development	+3	X	1	+3	X	3	=	+9
Chairperson County Medical Society	−1	X	3	−3	X	1	=	−3
Chairperson Black Medical Society	−1	X	3	−3	X	1	=	−3
Dean of Medical School	−2	X	3	−6	X	2	=	−12
Director City-County Public Health Department	−1	X	2	−2	X	0	=	0
Mayor	+1	X	3	+3	X	3	=	+9
Antipoverty Council	+3	X	1	+3	X	3	=	+9
Total	+8			+4				+30

under a citizens' group representing Middle City leadership, and not necessarily under the total auspices of the health service, seemed feasible.

This new information changed the issue I faced. The issue as now stated was that there be no overt opposition to the Neighborhood Health Center. With this issue, the political strategy was shaped. It dealt with not necessarily getting commitment from people but with neutralizing the opposition. With this in mind I began to compile a new list of actors. I replaced Dr. Goodguy, who was taking a sabbatical from the community at this point, with myself. Dr. Esteem, having been identified as a valuable support, was the next actor. Following him came the chairperson of the CCHD (under very low profile), the chairperson of the County Medical Society, the chairperson of the Black Medical Society, the Dean of the Medical School, and the director of the City-County Public Health Department. The mayor was also included as an actor. I asked the mayor's executive assistant for federal affairs to convince the mayor of the political advantage of claiming responsibility for the infusion of several million dollars a year into the community as evidence of the progress being made under his administration. In addition, I also involved the Neighborhood Antipoverty Council composed of poor residents of the area in which the Neighborhood Health Center was to be established.

After filling in and adding additional actors and eliminating one, I recalculated the issue positions (see Chart 9–3). I gave myself a +3. I previously mentioned my anger at discovering there was opposition to the neighborhood health facility, for which there were funds available. Consequently, I took a position I have rarely taken in my career, that of total support for a particular issue. Dr. Esteem's issue position came to +3 at this point, mainly because of the hoop-la that was being created in the community and the negative reaction toward Dr. Goodguy, which helped his issue position.

I then began to interact with the other major actors. I began to hold a series of lunches with the chairperson of the County Medical Society. During these I learned he was, in fact, still opposed to the idea, and his issue position ranked a –1. On the other hand, he did not have a closed mind and did not appear completely opposed to the Neighborhood Health Center after I explained the rationale of health services for the poor.

I also began to interact with the Dean. At our first meeting I found out that he was against the issue mainly because of his personal dislike for Dr. Goodguy. He conceded that the idea of a Neighborhood Health Center represented a model of service-delivery that he might be able to endorse. This concession on his part came after he made what I considered to be a test of my mettle. As I was ushered into his office he pushed his chair back from his desk, stood up, walked up to me, and said, "No son of a bitch is going to tell me how to deliver health services in this community." Reciprocating, I took one step toward him and replied, "And no son of a bitch is going to tell me how to deliver services to the poor in this community." The tension was immediately relieved and we began to discuss business. I had done considerable planning to prepare myself for my first contact with the Dean, and I was prepared to meet an autocratic and tough operator. Now you know that I'm a social worker by trade. If I had not been prepared for an adversary contact, I might have responded with the standard social worker reaction, "Why are you hostile to me today?" Obviously, that question would have failed his test. The use of a tough demeanor engendered a situation of mutual respect.

With the Black Medical Society I created the opportunity to speak at one of their meetings. I did my best to explain objectively the values of the Neighborhood Health Center for meeting the health needs of the poor in the community. I carefully and diplomatically hinted that our Neighborhood Antipoverty Council might be distressed enough to respond if they became aware that the opposition of the Black Medical Society was irreversible.

The director of the Public Health Department was extremely difficult to deal with. On the basis of our previous interaction I found I could not sway his opinion. My only means of reaching him was to state the case and give him time to think it over and make a decision. On the other hand, I knew he was an appointee of the mayor. The mayor's executive assistant had obtained the mayor's involvement in the issue, so I felt that the mayor would help eliminate the opposition of this member of his staff. The mayor's issue position was +1, while the director of Public Health Service was still –1. The chairperson of the Citizens' Committee for Human Development was still a +3, and, of course, we added the Neighborhood Antipoverty Council, which was staffed by persons employed by my agency. The council's issue position was amazingly similar to mine, +3. If we add up the column of issue positions (see Chart 9-3), we now find the sum is +8, which is a little stronger in favor of the issue than the first analysis of the initial PRINCE chart.

I then began to calculate the power, to see how this factor might affect the outcome of the decision. I gave myself power of 1 because I really could not influence the actors to change their minds and issue positions. My only asset was a reasonable amount of personal energy. Dr. Esteem still had a power position of 2, the chairperson of the Black Medical Society 3, and the director of the City-County Public Health Department 2. I gave the mayor a power of 3 in this situation because he potentially could command the behavior of the director of the City-County Public Health Department. The CCHD and the Antipoverty Council also had power of 1. If we multiply those factors and total the product column, the outcome is a +4. This is a substantial change from the –4 of the first PRINCE chart.

With the introduction of the salience factor, insights as to the resolution of the issue became clear. I, the Old Pro, was completely committed to this idea and my salience was 3. I threw in whatever energies I could muster in talking with people, cajoling people, and planning and plotting the positive outcome of this issue. I devoted almost two and a half months of my working schedule on nearly a full-time basis. To reduce potential error, I wrote three-quarters of the ultimate proposal myself and hand delivered it to Washington. Dr. Esteem's salience still remained at 1. He was a cool, relaxed character, and was involved in other important issues. It is interesting to note that my intervention with the chairperson of the County Medical Society lowered his salience. With Dr. Goodguy not on the scene, his resistance to an outsider was removed. He found out that the Antipoverty Council was not composed of wild-eyed radicals, so that if the center came into being, there would not be a horrendous upheaval in the community. Basically his new position was that although still against the idea of providing free health services, he could not, as a community leader, stand in the way of a project that might lead to improved health care for the disadvantaged. Likewise, my interaction with the Dean provided him with a person with whom he could do business. He admitted his approval of this particular form of health care delivery and agreed to support the idea. The salience of the Black Medical Society was reduced to 1 because the younger physicians took an increasingly vocal position in favor of the Neighborhood Health Center and the older black physicians elected not to voice their opposition. Both the mayor's executive assistant and I spent quite a bit of time working with the mayor to show him the importance of the Neighborhood Health Center and its public relations benefit for his administration. The mayor also instructed the director of the City-County Department of Public Health to withdraw his opposition. With these actions, I gave the mayor a salience of 3 and the director of the City-County Health Department zero. In fact, this eliminated the director as an actor. Finishing the multiplication, we find that the Old Pro had a total support of +9, Dr. Esteem +12, the chairperson of the County Medical Society -3, the Dean -12, the chairperson of the Black Medical Society -3, the mayor +9, the director of the City-County Department of Public Health a 0, the Citizens' Committee on Human Development a +9, and the Antipoverty Council +9, making a grand total of +30.

Today I am happy to announce that a Neighborhood Health Center has been established in Middle City. I was able to work with community leaders to assure that Dr. Goodguy became its first director (the reward for his low profile).

Section Three
The Culmination

Being a report from the boys and girls in the research and development section of the PRINCEtitute, Inc. on the ways to use the PRINCE system methods of collecting information, using the PRINCiples, and working with groups are described. The Appendixes show how to explore strategies with a boardgame and a computer model.

How to Get Data for Your Own PRINCE Analysis

10

A question that should have been gnawing at you as you read through the different applications of the PRINCE political accounting system is, "How the devil can I get the numbers for those charts?" After all, we are not dealing with the economy, where the price system neatly transforms all the important information into numerical terms. We are not going to lull you into a false sense of security by telling you that there is no problem. One of the most difficult tasks you must face in using this political accounting system is to come up with the numbers for the charts. The point to remember is this: You are making estimates of how people relate to you and to each other. Numbers used in research and problem solving by everybody—physicists, economists, generals—are also estimates. You will naturally want to make your estimates as carefully as possible. In the preceding chapters we hope we have given you some suggestions for making better estimates. But if you feel that what you are putting down on paper is only an approximation of what the world is "really" like—congratulations! You are in the very good company of scientists and scholars who deep in their hearts feel the same way, but who are rarely called upon to admit it openly. In a more positive sense, you are in good company as well because, like the scientist, what you lose in detail about each feeling of each element you consider, you will more than likely gain in usable knowledge about overall patterns and possibilities in the world around you.

There are, as a matter of fact, lots of social science techniques for transforming people's feelings and capabilities into numbers that can be used in the PRINCE charts. If you have access to opinion polls or other systematically gathered information, you should really be able to swing PRINCE. But we are not going to assume that you are always in such a happy condition. Even Dr. Gallup himself is liable to be caught in situations where he has to make spur-of-the-moment applications of PRINCE.

This chapter presents three ways of collecting information for PRINCE charts. First, we will discuss informal methods where you have neither the time nor the opportunity to use research tools. Second, we will discuss ways you can derive information from written materials. Third, we will provide a survey instrument that can be used on experts or on participants in the political process. Each approach has its strengths and limitations, but a knowledge of all three will go a long way toward answering the data question.

Some Informal Methods of Collecting Information

Obviously there are some general guidelines you can follow when filling in each of the charts. For the issue positions of the actors, read and listen to what they have said about the issue. Of course, you cannot take what they have said at face value, so check what they say for consistency and always take into account the audience to whom they are talking. Even here the chart will help you because you can assume that, when one political actor is talking to another, his issue position will appear closer to the target of his remarks than it really is. Let's go back to the family we met in Chapter 2. Father will not be as adamant about mother's desire to go bowling with the girls when he is talking to sister as he would be when he is talking to brother (see Chart 2-1). Use your common sense in figuring out where people stand and you will probably not miss very much.

For the power of political actors on issues, you need only ask yourself the question, "Who has the resources to stop an event from taking place or to make an event occur?" Mother may control the purse-strings, but father manages the budget. That is why those two in our example have so much power over the money issues. In more complicated political settings, power is much more diffused. Congress controls the purse-strings, but the executive branch has the capacity to act. In fact, it is precisely because power is generally diffused that the essence of politics is collective action. If one person could do anything he or she wanted, there would be no need for a political accounting system.

For the salience of the issue for each political actor, the task is not very difficult. The frequency with which an actor talks about the subject is a clear indication of his interest in it. We can also assume that the more things somebody wants, the less intense he feels about any one of them. Measurement gets a little complicated when we start talking about groups. In a group—whether it be the Kiwanis Club or the Democratic party—the leadership acts for the group. However, the salience the leadership feels for particular issues is directly related to the actual or anticipated awareness and feeling of the entire group. Hence, when nobody in the groups cares very much about an issue, the leaders probably do not attach much salience. However, if the rank and file become excited about it (or if there is a prospect they will become excited) the issue becomes the most important (salient) thing in the world for the leaders.

Of course, we are not denying the possibility that leaders may have strong opinions about issues even when they have rather low salience because their membership does not care about it very much. Leaders are simply more likely to act on the basis of their opinions when the followers care than when the followers do not care. It also scarcely needs to be mentioned that leaders will have a lot to say about what the rest of the group ignores or pays attention to. But they will rarely have monopoly control over salience, which is one of the reasons group leadership is so wearing—and politics is so interesting.

For the degree of friendship, neutrality, and hostility for a particular set of actors you must also frequently rely on judgment. Look at the tone and style of communications between any pair of political actors. Are they saying to each other, "Gee, we get along so well, why don't you do what I want?" Or are they saying, "If you don't do what I want, I'll never speak to you again." These two basic styles reflect real differences in feelings of friendship and hostility between the actors. When the mother in our PRINCE family says, "If you object to my bowling with the girls, I'll go home to mother," that's hostility. When the father says, "Sweetheart, because I bought a new suit, I'll do dishes for a month so you can go bowling on Thursday nights," that's friendship.

Of course you cannot always take the friendship-neutrality-hostility statements at face value. In some cases, friendly remarks and moderate discussions may cover seething hate. For that reason, it is necessary for you to examine closely the factors underlying the relationship between actors. Three such factors should be looked at in determining whether to assign a "+," "0," or "−" to the way one actor relates to another.

One reason for political friendship is that one actor feels morally or legally responsible to represent the interests and views of another actor. The most obvious case of this type of relationship is congressmen and voters in their districts. Similar cases can be found in the relationship between a supervisor and subordinates and a parent and his or her children. For our hypothetical family, Chart 2-6 indicates that both the father and mother have a feeling of political friendship for their son and daughter. This feeling is an example of political friendship based on a representational position.

A second reason for the existence of political friendship, neutrality, and hostility can be found in the mind set that has developed the historic patterns of agreement and disagreement over issues between two actors. Members of a political party in a legislature often agree with one another on a series of bills because in the past they have repeatedly found more on which to agree than to disagree. As a result they tend to be political friends. Conversely, members of opposing parties tend to disagree and tend therefore to be political enemies. Their hostility is a result of their historic disagreement with each other. In the family example, the father and grandmother are unfriendly to one another as a result of a long series of past disagreements on many issues (such as whether the marriage between the husband and wife should have taken place).

The final reason that friendship, neutrality, or hostility patterns develop between two actors is that one actor has something the other one wants. This situation is called "cross-issue bargaining." A legislature provides a convenient example. When a bill to support spending in one congressman's district is being considered, many different legislators will support it because they know that if they do, the legislator whose district is being helped is more likely to vote with them when a bill comes up to help their district. This so-called vote trading takes place in many different areas besides legislatures. In our family example you will note that the father and mother are friendly to each other. This is because the power of mother is high on issues salient to father and the power of father is high on issues salient to mother.

Providing estimations of political friendship, neutrality, and hostility between actors is a difficult task. First, you must ask if the relationship between the two actors is a result of some moral or legal obligation, if the relationship is determined by past agreements or disagreements, or if it is a result of a cross-issue bargaining relationship. Once this question is answered, you are prepared to determine whether a "+," "0," or "-" should go in the appropriate cell. If it is a moral or legal obligation, it should be a "+." If it is a result of consistency, the ratio of agreement to disagreement over the range of past and present issues affecting the two actors determines whether it is a "+," "0," or "-." If it is cross-issue bargaining, the relative power and salience of the respective actors determines whether it is a "+," or a "0." Precise calculations exist for making these determinations, but a computer is required to carry them out.* For most of your purposes, you can use the general rules to determine political friendship, neutrality, or hostility summarized below:

*See the PROBE model discussed in Chapter 14.

1. If there is a moral or legal obligation, then "+."
2. If past and present issues shape the relationship, then
   a. disagreement more than agreement, "–"
   b. agreement more than disagreement, "+"
   c. relative balance between agreement and disagreement, "0."
3. If there is cross-issue bargaining, then
   a. salience of actor is greater than power of other actor, "+"
   b. salience of actor is equal to or less than power of other actor, "0."

Although extremely complex to complete, the chart showing the relationships among political actors is important. By understanding these relationships in terms of the friendship-neutrality-hostility concepts we have described above, you can determine the propensity one actor has to agree with another regardless of the original actor's predisposition. For example, we would expect that father could get mother to agree with his positions on issues more readily than most other family members. These patterns are relatively stable and therefore can be used to forecast the degree to which changes in issue position might occur.

Systematic Data Collection from
Documentary Sources

So far we have been discussing how to translate your general understanding of a political situation into the numbers, pluses, and minuses of the PRINCE charts. Many of the situations you will want to study will be situations in which you have a lot of general information, either because of your personal knowledge and involvement or because it is something you have carefully studied by reading books, magazine articles, and newspapers. Therefore, you will often find that you will be able to fill out the charts using the information you have. In analyzing such situations, you might use in an informal way some of the techniques discussed below.

However, you may want to do some new research and information gathering about a situation you don't have a lot of information about and gather the information as systematically as possible. The rest of this chapter has some pointers for doing this. Keep in mind, however, that even the most precise and systematic research will not help you unless you have a clear idea of what you are gathering the data on. Therefore, keep a clear idea of the first part of this chapter if you try any of the techniques suggested in this section.

Issue position. Public news stories and other accounts of political issues usually have a great deal of information about the IP's of actors. Participants in politics are frequently expressing themselves as being for or against various proposed courses of action. The more consistently an actor states publicly that he or she is for something, the more confidently you can assign a positive IP for that actor. Make sure, however, that the actor states his or her position consistently before many different audiences before you assign an IP. Also look for qualifications in an actor's support or opposition statements. In case no qualifications are ever mentioned, you can assign a +3 or a –3. Depending on how frequently qualifications are mentioned, you should assign a 2 or a 1.

In legislative bodies of various sorts, actors are often called upon to vote and explain their vote on various public issues. These votes can also frequently be used to assign IP's. In still other cases, you can estimate an actor's IP fairly closely simply by knowing the purpose of an intended decision. If its purpose is to make that actor richer, more important, or otherwise help the actor, you don't have to worry too much about assigning a positive IP to the actor on that issue. If, conversely, the decision has a likely result of being harmful to the actor's interests, a negative IP is a good bet.

Salience. Salience is a trickier thing to measure. One thing to look for is how frequently an actor says or does anything about the issue. The more activity, the more salient the issue probably is to that actor. Somewhat paradoxically, a lack of activity may sometimes indicate high salience.

The effect on the actor can also be a clue to salience. The more an actor's interests are affected by a proposed decision, the more salient it will normally be to him. For example, a minimum wage law is generally high salience to a labor union. However, much more salient would be a proposed law designed to affect the right to strike, which affects the very *raison d'être* of a labor union.

Power. Power is difficult to measure, but it is the most constant, or slowly changing, component of the PRINCE system. Generally speaking, current reports on the dynamics of political situations do not explicitly give information about power.

In order to estimate power, you will most likely have to do some background research on the attributes and position of an actor. Does the actor possess many resources that are important in determining the way a decision is made? For example, does he or she control committees, sources of communication, or other important institutions? If the decision has to do with money, does the actor have a lot of wealth? If the decision has to do with possible coercion, does the actor possess a lot of capacity for coercion? Be very careful here to avoid the "halo effect" that is a weakness in many political analyses. Just because an actor possesses a lot of one kind of resource doesn't mean he or she is powerful on all issues. The United States, for example, possesses an overwhelming military power with respect to Canada, but this hasn't stopped the Canadians from putting severe restrictions on American investments in their economy.

In trying to measure any of these three variables, issue position, salience, and power, you should develop a list as you go through your sources. Make a note of each instance of evidence about one of the three variables. Then put all the actors in rank order, with the highest on top and the lowest on the bottom. After doing this, you can usually decide with a fair degree of confidence which ones to assign a 3, which a 2, which a 1, and which a 0.

Friendship-neutrality-hostility. In deciding what scores to give actors for this chart, history is sometimes a good source. It may tell you if the two actors usually cooperate or conflict, and therefore whether to assign a "+" or a "–" between them. It *usually* happens that the way the first actor feels about the second is the way the second will feel about the first. But look out for exceptions to this. Although they are rather infrequent, exceptions can be extremely important as a clue to future issue positions.

The sources you use for the other variables will sometimes also contain information about friendly relations between two actors, or even formal pacts and alliances. This can be very useful in filling out the friendship-neutrality-hostility chart.

Acquiring PRINCE Data from a Survey

Sometimes it is not easy to find issue position, power, salience, or friendship-neutrality-hostility from documentary sources. In this case you might resort to interviewing experts such as journalists, governmental officials, or academics who have studied the actor extensively. You might also try interviewing the actors, but you will probably have a very difficult time because information on their issue position, power, salience, or friendship-neutrality-hostility (or even perceptions of other's views) is more sacred than any other information at their disposal. If it is not, then the actor is either not very smart or not very important.

We should also mention at the outset that the procedure described below can be used on yourself to help you formulate questions you might ask informally or through your documentary research. In this way, you would be using the survey to provide guidance in your search for information. Even though the survey procedure described below is designed primarily to be used on experts, you might find it helpful for other purposes.

Before going to interview each expert, you should prepare an index card with the issue on which you are seeking information. Use a separate index card for each issue. Identify each issue on the card with a letter of the alphabet. For example, if you have five issues, the cards should be lettered A through E.

To record the data, you could reproduce the form on the following pages. Be sure to explain each of the concepts clearly to the experts. You should have them clearly in your own mind before doing the research. Also make certain that the experts understand how they are to complete the scale.

On the following pages we have reproduced a sample survey instrument for use with five decisions. You may design a similar instrument with more outputs for your own use if it is necessary.

You should also have your respondent fill out the friendship-neutrality-hostility form for as many of the actors as he or she has information about. Note that if you are doing a paper-and-pencil PRINCE analysis, all you will need is the "+," "0," or "−" for each response. If you are doing a PROBE analysis you will also want the "Because" information. A "1" is an indication of interest aggregation; a "2" is an indication of consistency; and a "3" is an indication of cross-issue bargaining.

Sample Survey Instrument

Questionnaire Concerning ————————————————————
(name of actor)

Name   ————————————————————————————
(name of respondent)

Date Questionnaire Completed ————————————————

Please read through this questionnaire before you begin to supply any of the requested information. If you have any questions about the meaning of terms or the procedures to be used, ask the administrator before you begin.

Note that on each card one output is stated in terms of a specific outcome. Also note that each card has a letter printed in the upper left-hand corner. When you fill out the questionnaire, use only those identifying letters and not the verbal descriptions of the issues. You are requested to supply data on issue position, power, and salience for the actor listed above for each of the circled outputs on the questionnaire.

Remember that you are not to rate yourself on these outputs. Neither are you to pretend that you are the actor named above. Rather, on the basis of your knowledge and judgment about the actor, you are to estimate to the best of your ability the proper scores on each of the variables.

Score of Issue Position

Issue position is the stance of an actor of support for, opposition to, or neutrality toward an issue. An issue is a potential decision (typically favored by some and opposed by others) that involves the allocation of some value by a decision maker.

You are requested to estimate the actor's issue position on each of the outputs circled below. Issue position is measured on a scale ranging from –3 to +3 where the –3 endpoint signifies extremely firm opposition to the proposed issue, 0 represents neutrality, and the +3 endpoint signifies extremely firm support. Circle the point on the scale that best indicates the actor's issue position. Please check the questionnaire before returning it to make certain that you have circled a score for each of the circled issues on the left and that you have not circled more than one score for a particular issue.

Output

A –1 Slightly firm opposition   0   +1 Slightly firm support
    –2 Moderately firm opposition Neutral +2 Moderately firm support
    –3 Extremely firm opposition   +3 Extremely firm support

B –1 Slightly firm opposition   0   +1 Slightly firm support
    –2 Moderately firm opposition Neutral +2 Moderately firm support
    –3 Extremely firm opposition   +3 Extremely firm support

C –1 Slightly firm opposition   0   +1 Slightly firm support
    –2 Moderately firm opposition Neutral +2 Moderately firm support
    –3 Extremely firm opposition   +3 Extremely firm support

D –1 Slightly firm opposition   0   +1 Slightly firm support
    –2 Moderately firm opposition Neutral +2 Moderately firm support
    –3 Extremely firm opposition   +3 Extremely firm support

E –1 Slightly firm opposition   0   +1 Slightly firm support
    –2 Moderately firm opposition Neutral +2 Moderately firm support
    –3 Extremely firm opposition   +3 Extremely firm support

Score of Salience

Salience is the importance of the issue to an actor. It is measured on a scale that ranges from 0 to 3; 0 signifies not important, and 3 signifies extremely important.

You are requested to estimate the actor's salience score for each of the issues circled below. Circle the point on the scale that best indicates the actor's salience score. Please check the questionnaire before returning it to make certain that you have circled a score for each of the circled issues on the left and that you have not circled more than one score for a particular issue.

Output

A (0) Not at all important   (1) Slightly important   (2) Moderately important   (3) Extremely important

B (0) Not at all important   (1) Slightly important   (2) Moderately important   (3) Extremely important

C (0) Not at all important   (1) Slightly important   (2) Moderately important   (3) Extremely important

D (0) Not at all important   (1) Slightly important   (2) Moderately important   (3) Extremely important

E (0) Not at all important   (1) Slightly important   (2) Moderately important   (3) Extremely important

Score of Power

Power is the relative capacity possessed by a given actor to do one of two things: either to affect the likelihood of an issue taking place or to have an effect on the relationship between a given decision and its intended outcome. In other words, an actor may be capable of either blocking the positive decision on an issue or making it occur as intended.

You are asked to assign a value for the actor's power on each of the circled issues. Power ranges from 0 to 3 where 0 signifies no power to affect the outcome and 3 represents a very great capacity to affect the outcome. Circle the point on the scale that best represents the actor's power score on that issue. Before returning the questionnaire, check to make certain that you have assigned a power value for each of the circled issues and that you have not circled more than one score for a particular issue.

Output

A (0) Not at all powerful   (1) Slightly powerful   (2) Moderately
powerful   (3) Extremely powerful
B (0) Not at all powerful   (1) Slightly powerful   (2) Moderately
powerful   (3) Extremely powerful
C (0) Not at all powerful   (1) Slightly powerful   (2) Moderately
powerful   (3) Extremely powerful
D (0) Not at all powerful   (1) Slightly powerful   (2) Moderately
powerful   (3) Extremely powerful
E (0) Not at all powerful   (1) Slightly powerful   (2) Moderately
powerful   (3) Extremely powerful

Friendship-Neutrality-Hostility

Now I would like some information about how each actor is likely to deal with each other actor concerning the issues we are studying. For each pair of actors, whose names are entered in the blanks, please indicate with a check mark: (1) whether the first-named actor in question is likely to be friendly, neutral, or hostile toward the second actor and (2) what is the reason for the friendship, neutrality, or hostility.

1. ————————— is likely to ——— (+) be friendly to
(0) be neutral to
(-) be hostile to ——————

Because the first-named actor:
——————— (1) feels him- or herself to be a representative of the second
actor.
——————— (2) has a historical and/or general pattern of agreement or
disagreement with the second actor.
——————— (3) feels that it would be advantageous to strike a bargain
with the second actor.

Of course, many research projects will combine several different ways of getting information. In Appendix B, which describes the PROBE computer program, there is an example of a paper on the politics of international oil policy that uses both the questionnaire and other sources of information. You may want to look at it as an example of how to use different sources of information in your own PRINCE analysis, whether you do the analysis by hand or with a computer.

Summary of PRINCiples and Guidelines for Action

11

If you have thoroughly digested—and retained—what has been said in the previous pages, you are ready to apply the PRINCE accounting system to your own political problems. You may wish to apply the system in order to accomplish some definite goal or you may wish to use the system in order to have a better understanding of some political activity you are observing—to figure out why political actors act the way they do and why some succeed and some fail.

Taken by itself, this chapter is of no more use than a doctor's medical bag or a carpenter's tool chest is for someone who hasn't been allowed to train under the guidance of an experienced physician or journeyman carpenter. There is, of course, no formal licensing requirement that must be met before you can legally engage in the practice of politics. Whether there should be such a requirement is open to debate. If you look at some of the people who do practice politics, you may be inclined to think there should be restrictions, as they have in medicine— that is, until you look at some of the doctors. But in any event the preceding chapters do provide a substitute for the experience you would get if you had been able to follow on a first-hand basis the political activities of a United States congressman or a Machiavellian administrator. We must admit that the preceding pages are actually a poor substitute for such direct training. Experience is a uniquely valuable teacher in the skill of political problem solving as it is in most of life's tasks. It is also true, of course, that people can and do fail to learn from experience as well as from any other teachers. Without a systematic, careful observation of what's going on around you, experience is no help at all. Undoubtedly the best of both worlds is a systematic framework applied to actual experience. Besides, we all must learn to adapt to the realities of life, which in this case means using this book as at least a partial substitute for real experience.

In this chapter we assume that you are attempting to use some paper and pencil form of PRINCE analysis to formulate a political strategy for yourself. Subsequent chapters suggest group decision making, gaming, and computer procedures for applying the framework. Fortunately, the PRINCiples inserted throughout the chapters in the second section of this book provide guidelines for using the information in the PRINCE charts to formulate and execute political strategies. Before reviewing those PRINCiples, we would like to identify the four major prescriptions inherent in the PRINCE analysis system:

1. Get the actors to agree with your issue position.
2. Raise the salience for those actors on those issues for which they agree with you and lower the salience for those actors on those issues for which they disagree.
3. Contribute to the power of those actors who agree with your issue position(s) and try to reduce the power of those who do not.
4. Increase your friends and reduce your enemies.

This advice may seem obvious to you. If it does, you should be encouraged and may in fact be entitled to enroll in an advance level course at your neighborhood PRINCEtitute because it means that you have so thoroughly acquired PRINCE wisdom that profundities seem to be truisms. Regardless of the reasons, the four guidelines expressed above will not do you very much good by themselves because all politicians and all beneficiaries of PRINCE will be simultaneously tailoring their actions to fit the guidelines. Nevertheless, keep them in mind when designing and executing your strategy.

Many of the PRINCiples listed below speak to these four imperatives. Before examining them, however, we need to list those that have to do with the mechanics of the PRINCE analysis. These include:

3.2   Identify issues in terms of relatively specific outcomes.

4.1   Include actors relevant to your issue and issues relevant to those actors even if the issues are irrelevant to you.

8.2   Look for actors in the following general categories: governmental officials, party supporters, extracommunity actors, the legal system, and the mass media.

3.1   To simplify the PRINCE charts, lump together actors who have strong common interests.

3.3   Use the PRINCE system to project voting decisions of legislative bodies.

6.2   No matter how technical the public question, political factors must be considered important.

To get actors to agree with your issue position, the following PRINCiples are most relevant:

8.1   Exhaust all routine options before executing a political strategy.

7.8   One must always match the chances of success of various alternatives with the relative benefits that would result from the success.

4.2   Ideology should be a political tool, not a philosophical crutch. Don't let ideology determine all your issue positions.

3.6   Compromise occurs on issues about which there is no consensus if actors have a consensus on other issues.

3.5   Polarization is destructive and consensus is constructive if you are on the side of the consensus. If you are not, the converse is true.

7.5   If the purpose of a committee is to educate its members so they will change their issue position, the death of the committee might represent success.

6.1   When there are many competing interests focused on a single public policy, changes in policies tend to occur too late and be too extreme.

It should be noted that the PRINCiples 6.2, 8.1, and 7.8 have more to do with establishing your own issue position than with bargaining considerations to get others to change their position. This is because the choice of goals should always be done with an idea of how feasible those goals will be. We are not advocating that you choose feasible goals over unfeasible ones in every case, but we do feel strongly that you should think very carefully about the feasibility of the goals you choose.

To raise salience for those actors on those issues for which they agree with you and lower the salience for those actors on those issues for which they disagree with you, you should remember the following PRINCiples:

4.5   The mass media often controls the salience of issues for many actors, and what turns the mass media on is frequently not directly related to the issue.

5.1   Variation in salience on the same issue for two opposing actors is often interrelated.

5.2   The number of issues an actor can have high salience on is limited; introducing a new high salience issue may reduce the salience on other issues.

3.4   Always remember to consider salience when making a compromise. It's frequently prudent to offer a little extra to the side with the higher salience.

6.4   The poorer the actor, the higher the salience on growth issues.

6.3   As long as resources increase, political support can be maintained by adopting public policies that satisfy the most salient interest of each actor.

7.7   Bureaucrats use jargon and committees for the political purpose of keeping salience low.

To contribute to the power of those actors who agree with your issue positions and reduce the power of those who do not, the following PRINCiples are important:

4.3   In an increasingly complicated society, knowledge is important to establish an actor's power on an issue.

7.2   Technical knowledge must be used skillfully before it can give power to political actors.

7.3   Cooptation is a strategy required when one is dealing with more powerful actors.

8.3   Bureaucrats have little power over broad public policy questions; but they often have tremendous power vis-à-vis limited decisions that can be very important to individuals. Therefore, don't ignore them in your calculations.

7.1   Bureaucrats have to operate in a situation in which their power is low.

8.4   The degree to which power is centralized or decentralized among the political actors should shape your political strategies.

4.6   Changing power sometimes requires institutional change, which takes a very long time, but there may be no other alternative.

7.6   Access to actual actors is often difficult.

To use the friendship-neutrality-hostility charts effectively, the following PRINCiples may be helpful:

8.5   The patterns of friendship-neutrality-hostility among the political actors should shape your political strategies.

4.4   Ignore actors who want to be your political friends if those actors don't have any other friends or don't have power.

8.6   Use friendship-neutrality-hostility charts to decide who should exert influence to change issue positions.

7.4   Discuss procedure when there are strong differences among participants on a committee.

To further help you, we will describe three very different styles of strategy that you can choose in finding a PRINCE-based solution to your political problems. A brief word about the three styles should suffice.

The first and easily the most efficient is the strategy of *consensus*. You should follow this strategy when your PRINCE charts suggest that there is sufficient friendship among actors in the system to make deals and the likelihood for support for you and/or your policy positions (taking issue position, power, and salience into account) is high. Washington's classic manipulation of the Constitutional Convention illustrates how the consensus strategy can produce phenomenal success and Mortimer LaStrange's approach to the building of low-cost housing illustrates how a consensus strategy can yield highly limited success under conditions that are basically unfavorable.

Consensus strategy is what all experienced politicians like to pursue because it requires the smallest changes and therefore the fewest costs. It accepts the issue position, salience, and power of the actors and finds compromises and agreements through negotiation. It calls for no actions to change people's minds about the basic issues or to raise or lower their power or salience. It requires both luck and skill, but it is always worth a try.

When consensus strategy fails, one might try the strategy of *limited conflict*. This is a strategy in which you attempt to alter the salience, power, or issue position of a selected number of actors in hopes that you can sneak through with your objectives before all the actors in the system get thoroughly involved. It is a strategy of focused pressure, similar to Nader's attempt to raise salience on the auto issue. You use the strategy when you discover one or two critical actors who can change the system from hopeless inaction to quiet but effective action. If Ryan, the dentist with the tax problem, could have raised the salience of his councilman or of the courts, he could have had his change without a lot of commotion. Limited conflict can best yield results in situations where there is basic friendliness among actors and someone vulnerable to pressure.

Although it costs more in terms of time and effort than the consensus approach because it requires changes in issue position, salience, or power of some of the actors, a limited-conflict strategy is frequently required. It is usually necessary for individuals who are seeking to get concerted action from a group or a government for a specific private or public interest. Depending upon your goals, it is also often required in dealing with broad group decisions and elections. Needless to say, the strategy of limited conflict has its costs, but it also has its possible rewards.

There are times when neither the strategy of consensus nor the strategy of limited conflict will work. At such times, the political actor is forced to choose between two rather costly alternatives. The first is the alternative of *changing the distribution of power among the relevant actors*. Such a change can only occur over an extended period of time and through hard work. It can take the form of developing party organizations, registering disenfranchised voters, and motivating those who have latent power (e.g., the wealthy) to use it. Sometimes, changing economic or social conditions can produce a political windfall by altering voting patterns. Or one can hope that a new generation of business, civic, and governmental leaders will be different from the old. No matter what the process, however, the strategy of winning through an alteration in power takes the kind of patience and strength possessed by very few political actors.

Lacking that patience and strength, political actors who are unsuccessful with the consensus and limited conflict strategies sometimes choose the alternative of *unlimited conflict* or, to be poetic, "total war." This is a strategy in which you attempt to raise the salience of every issue, not only your particular issue but also all of the other issues in the system. You do this in order to establish a potential bargaining position with the other actors and also to create stagnation in the political system. If you can succeed in raising everyone's salience on all issues, you will stymie political decisions because the spotlight of salience will throw in sharper relief the differences, which in turn will obscure the basis for cooperation.

The record of unlimited conflict as a strategy is not very encouraging, however. Whether we are talking about wars between nations, civil wars, all-out fights in Congress, or a family argument that covers every issue, very few initiators of unlimited conflict gain what they were after when they started the conflict. Bobby Planter lost, and Ralph Nader would have lost if he had decided to fight all the political actors on all the inequities of the system. Unless the actor has a large preponderance of power (and in that case, he would not have to pursue a strategy of unlimited conflict), the prospect of political success from such a strategy is quite low.

One should distinguish, however, the *strategy* of unlimited conflict from the *threat* of unlimited conflict. Occasionally such a threat works, as it did for Hitler in 1938, students in the late 1960s and early 1970s, and for some senators when they threaten filibusters. The threat of total conflict is inherent in many successful political strategies, even though eventually the bluff is called or all the actors start making threats so that the strategy's effectiveness wanes. Threatening to bargain on every issue as if it were a life-and-death matter can be a moderately successful, very high-risk strategy.

But the *actual* strategy of unlimited conflict in contrast to its threat almost never produces success. The reason for this is easily understood in PRINCE terms. A strategy of unlimited conflict means that all actors see all issues as highly salient because they are tied to the question of the survival of either themselves or the political system in which they are operating. During the cold war period, for example, Russia and the United States saw all issues ranging from Berlin to who had the best ballet company as occasions for conflict. The American Civil War was a product not just of the debate over slavery but the fear in the South that the North would oppose all southern issue positions. In an all-out battle between the mayor's office and the city council, every budget item becomes symbolic of the battle itself. To give an inch on some irrelevant issue in a high-conflict situation is viewed by both sides as tantamount to giving a mile. Although such conflicts cannot last indefinitely, they do occur in such a way that the original aims of the actors become lost in the concern for victory and dominance.

This is why a strategy that calls even for the threat of unlimited conflict (as opposed to the unlimited conflict itself) is so dangerous. The teachers in a school district may start out negotiations with the school board by saying that they refuse to accept any points of the initial offer in order to establish a bargaining position. If the school board takes them seriously, a six-month strike and even violence could ensue. Sometimes the threats of total conflict are ritualized so that the threatened party knows that the threatening party is merely establishing a bargaining position. However, in situations where there is already a great deal of hostility among the actors and growing polarization between groups of actors, the threat of unlimited conflict can lead directly to unlimited conflict itself, and the winners will certainly *not* be the parties who start the conflict in the first place.

This is not to say that there will be no winners. If unlimited conflict as a threat and as a strategy occurs in politics, there must be some reason for it. Despite the low success rate and high cost of such conflict, it does occur. Who benefits? The answer is those people who are so frustrated with their failures—real or imagined and related or unrelated to the issues—that they adopt the strategy as their psychological payoffs. The term *alienation* sums up the phenomenon quite well. For real or imagined reasons, political actors have been known to pursue the path of unlimited conflict even though they often acknowledged the self-destructive nature of that strategy.

But the winners are not just the kooks. Sometimes "normal" actors capitalize on the total conflict strategies of others. Both the American military-industrial complex and the educational system benefited tremendously during the 1950s from the cold war strategy followed by the United States. Moderate liberals in the cities and on the campuses have gained in recent years from the all-out strategies of the SDS and the Black Panthers. Widgit-producing countries also gained in their conflict with country I. The benefits derived help to sustain the unlimited conflict strategies even though those who pursue those strategies usually only receive psychic rewards.

Needless to say, we refuse to advocate the unlimited conflict strategy or even to suggest that you employ the threat of unlimited conflict— save for extremely serious occasions—as an approved PRINCE method of solving political problems. We have mentioned it here so that you recognize it when you see it and stop yourself from undertaking it, unless of course your problem is the psychological need for political destruction. Ultimately, we hope that the dissemination of the PRINCE approach throughout the world will obviate the political alienation that generates the strategy of unlimited conflict. When that day comes, the PRINCE method for solving political problems will become the PRINCE path to justice, freedom, and world peace.

Group Decision Making and Group Therapy

12

Throughout this book we have emphasized how individuals can use the PRINCE system to make political decisions. Recent advances growing out of the urban laboratory of PRINCEtitute, Inc. suggest that when a group of people who have the same purpose attempt to formulate a plan for political action, they can employ the PRINCE accounting system collectively. For example, the professional staff of a community bureaucracy such as a housing authority or sanitation department might want to determine a strategy for achieving a policy objective that involves an executive action of a mayor or the passing of a law by the local legislature.

In the sections that follow we are assuming that groups will use the PRINCE system as outlined so far—that is, within manual calculations. There are times when a problem involves so many actors and issues that this becomes impossible. For problems of this sort it becomes necessary to program a computer to carry out the calculations. The PRINCEtitute has, in fact, written such programs. But for most problems hand calculations are fully sufficient.

For a group to use the PRINCE system to aid in decision making, we suggest the following steps:

1. Outline four empty PRINCE charts on a large blackboard and purchase a gallon of wine. Both items are required to facilitate communications. (Or, as the old Latin saying has it, *in vino, PRINCEtas.*) The members of the group should meet about three hours.

139

2. Make sure that all members of the group are familiar with the PRINCE system for solving political problems.

3. Define the one or more policy outcomes the group would like to see achieved. (*Note:* If the group cannot agree on this list, it is not ready to participate in the exercise. It must in fact take part in a group therapy session that will be described in the next section.)

4. As the policy outcomes are defined, they should be entered in the issue position, power, and salience charts for primary analysis.

5. The group should then define the most important actors. The whole range of actors should be defined, including voting blocs, political figures, bureaucrats—whoever is defined by group members as relevant actors. (*Note:* Consensus is not so crucial here because the actors suggested by every member of the group can be listed initially, with streamlining to follow later.)

6. Once the last of the actors has been determined and the primary issues identified, the group should attempt to estimate the issue position, power, and salience of each of the actors. Here is where the tremendous analytic powers of the PRINCE system take their effect. Debate among members of the group over whether, for example, actor #3 is a -2 or +1 will involve the group in articulating and mutually exploring their collective view of the world. If disagreements persist after a thorough discussion of each value and it is not clear which members in the dialogue are either correct or more powerful, the situation can be analyzed more than once using the different values each time.

7. Following the completion of the three charts on the primary issue, a friendship-neutrality-hostility chart for all the actors should be constructed. Again, members of the group should be encouraged to debate over the proper values for particular friendship-neutrality-hostility scores. This dialogue can be extremely helpful in bringing as much systematic analysis to bear on the description of the political environment with which the group must deal.

8. Once these charts are completed, what remains to be done is to explore the strategic alternatives suggested by the data in the charts. All of the rules of strategy presented throughout this book should be brought into the discussion. The desirability of consensus, limited conflict, or all-out conflict strategies should be explored along with the advisability of such tactics as those performed by George Washington, Ralph Nader, and Mortimer LaStrange.

9. In analyzing the situation, the question of what other issues

should be entered into the chart can be explored. If a strategy of bargaining is indicated, issues other than the primary ones might be included. The strategy might be to get the backing of a given actor by supporting his issue position or, conversely, threatening to withdraw support from it. To do this effectively, the group should add to the list some issues that other actors in the charts think are important. Your group may get a concession from group A by changing its issue position to satisfy group A when such a change will cost your group the support it already has from group B. Nevertheless, by charting the issues most relevant to the actors you have identified, you will be able to plan an effective bargaining strategy (assuming of course your group has enough power to make its threats and promises mean something).

Group Therapy

In the previous section, we discussed how a group can use the PRINCE system to solve problems in its political environment. We also mentioned the possibility that the group itself may not have its collective head together. This can be easily discovered when the members of the group disagree on the definition of the issues as well as the support or opposition their group should have for particular policy outcomes. Such disagreement shows that the members of the group have sufficiently different issue positions and saliences that they cannot decide on mutually acceptable group goals.

We suggest the following procedure:

1. Reproduce four empty PRINCE charts on a blackboard and purchase *two* gallons of wine. The members of the group should meet at least three hours. Under some conditions, longer meetings are required.

2. Each member of the group should be identified as an actor and should present his view of the four most important issues that confront the group. These issues may have to do with the leadership of the group, the actions the group should take or even when or where the group should meet.

3. Each actor should then fill in his issue position, salience, and power as well as his feelings of hostility and friendship for the other members of the group. When the charts are completed, there should be a search for areas of agreement. Usually, the members of the group will state their positions in a relatively moderate way so that the charts will indicate more consensus than there actually is. Even taking this into

account, the members may find some genuine examples of reasonableness of other members. This can help initiate cooperation among members of the group that can last anywhere from two days to six months.

4. We recommend that the group move right into a problem-solving exercise immediately after this therapy session. Such a move will remind the group that they are collectively faced with a troublesome outside environment. This will hinder the growth of the virus of dissension that may have not been thoroughly eliminated through the therapy session.

We might mention that this application has proven to be very effective in building consensus in all types of social and governmental groups. In groups and situations where dissent grows like topsy, the PRINCEtitute, Inc. recommends periodic group therapy sessions.

To help you visualize what we have in mind, reflect on the family situation provided in Chapter 2. If the father, mother, sister, brother, and grandmother had gotten together in front of five empty PRINCE charts, they would have been able to discover where they agreed and disagreed. Remember, they probably would have softened their views somewhat so that the disagreement over issues did not look irreconcilable and the friendship-neutrality-hostility chart did not look so much like a representation of a soap opera family.

The staff psychologists of the PRINCEtitute are unanimous in their belief that when any group exchanges ideas about their feelings toward a set of common problems (especially when the members constitute problems for one another) the result is a psychologically beneficial clearing of the air. The PRINCE system takes advantage of this conclusion by constituting a simple, straightforward framework within which such exchanges can take place.

Even if the PRINCE charts were completed honestly by the members of the family, there would still be hope, because the emotional experience of being honest would probably lessen the hostility level. In effect, what we have suggested is *structured* sensitivity training, something as revolutionary as sensitivity training once was. By letting it all hang out in the PRINCE charts, the members of the family would feel cleansed by the fresh air of structured truth. Although the family members may feel bruised, the long-range effect would be a more open honest set of relationships.

Any group of actors having disagreement over basic issues would benefit by taking part in regular sessions of PRINCE therapy. Professional staffs within government and industry, boards of directors, and members of executive agencies should periodically get together to define the issues dividing their group and complete the issue position, power, salience, and friendship-neutrality-hostility charts. Congressional committees and subcommittees might even find the exercise worthwhile, particularly if they could learn to provide honest information on their issue positions, power, salience, and friendship-neutrality-hostility. Such a suggestion, however, is based on the impossible hope that honesty and rationality become norms of the political system, and we offer it only as an illustrative point.

Conducting PRINCE Political Analyses in Groups

You may find the following guidelines useful in conducting PRINCE political analysis sessions when more than two individuals are working together. For group sessions, we suggest that you do one issue at a time and use the Mini-PRINCE issue analysis form appearing at the end of this chapter.

Summary of Estimates to Be Made

Issue position. How each actor feels about the issue-outcome under study. It ranges from +3 for strong support, through 0 for neutrality, to –3 for strong opposition.

Power. How much usable capability each actor has to affect the outcome. It ranges from 0 for no power to 3 for maximum power.

Salience. How important is the issue to the actor. How much of the actor's agenda is taken up with this issue. It ranges from 0 for no importance to 3 for maximum importance.

Friendship-neutrality-hostility. What is the general feeling each actor has for each of the others. It ranges from +3 for strong friendship, through 0 for indifference, to –3 for strong hostility.

Some Steps to Keep in Mind

1. Be sure the issue you are dealing with is very specifically defined and all members of the group fully understand the definition. Remember that the issue must be defined in terms of an observable outcome that some people will want to have happen and others will want

to prevent. It may turn out that in trying to define an issue-outcome you will discover that you are actually talking of several different possible outcomes. If this happens, try to get agreement to analyze one of the issues and later cover others if there is time. Members may submit minority PRINCE reports if they wish.

2. After formulating an agreed-upon statement of the issue, engage in general group discussion to develop a preliminary partial listing of the relevant actors. At this point keep the list of actors small, probably no more than ten should be included. Make sure that all group members understand clearly who all of the actors are—they should be identified as clearly and specifically as the issues.

3. After the preliminary list of actors has been agreed upon, assign an actor to each member of the group. (Two members can deal with one actor or one member may deal with two actors, depending upon the group size.) Take a few minutes while each group member works independently to estimate the actor's issue position, power, and salience on the issue, and also to estimate the relative friendship-neutrality-hostility sent to each of the other actors and received from them.

4. After this has been done, have the group member responsible give his or her estimates for the issue position, power, and salience of the first listed actor. Follow this with general discussion to develop group consensus on the estimates for that actor. Follow the same procedure for each actor.

5. After the issue position, power, and salience have been estimated, follow the same procedure for the friendship-neutrality-hostility estimates.

6. When the charts have been filled in, complete the issue-outcome calculations. Multiply issue position times power times salience for each actor. Add the resulting numbers, being careful to include the positive and negative numbers correctly.

7. If the resulting number is a large positive number (above +5) the prediction is that your issue is likely to occur; if the number is a large negative number (below −5) the issue is very unlikely to occur; if the number is close to zero, the prospect for the issue is fifty-fifty.

8. If you feel that the number you have achieved is unreasonable (either too positive or too negative), go over the charts again to see if you would revise your estimates. You should also consider whether you have left out one or two actors whose scores would make substantial differences in the predicted outcome.

Mini-PRINCE Issue Analysis Form

This form is to be used when an individual or group wishes to acquire a quick understanding of a single political issue. Prior to the implementation of strategies developed under the PRINCE political accounting system, we suggest the longer analysis be performed.

Issue: _____

(State in terms of a desired political outcome)

Actors	Issue position	X	Power	X	Salience	=	Total support by actor
		X		X		=	
		X		X		=	
		X		X		=	
		X		X		=	
		X		X		=	
		X		X		=	
		X		X		=	
		X		X		=	
		X		X		=	
		X		X		=	
					Total for all actors =		

Thomas A. O'Donnell

PRINCEdown 2: A Game of Political Strategies[*]

Appendix A

PRINCEdown 2, A Game of Political Strategies, is described in this chapter for those wishing to analyze and evaluate alternative political strategies through the medium of political gaming. The game is based on the same information used in PRINCE charts, which is put into an adaptation of the PRINCE charts called a PRINCEdown 2 Profile (P2P). Just as the PRINCE chart describes a political situation, the P2P sets the stage at the start of the game on the basis of which the bargaining in PRINCEdown 2 takes place. This chapter describes materials you will need to play the game, the rules of the bargaining, how to make a P2P to play a game with your own set of issues, and how to analyze the results of the play to help you evaluate alternative political strategies.

Directions for Playing PRINCEdown 2

In this section, we will briefly describe how you set up the game, the activities in each cycle, and the scoring. Before doing that, however, we should say something about the purpose of the game and the goals you should seek in playing the game. The purpose of PRINCEdown 2 is to explore strategies you might want to follow or advocate following in real-life situations. Hence, it is imperative that all of the players remain

*The original version of PRINCEdown, authored by William D. Coplin, Michael O'Leary, and Stephen Mills, was the source of some of the material used in this version. However, PRINCEdown 2 is a thoroughly revised version developed and field tested by the author.

faithful to the roles they ascribe to the actors they are playing throughout the exercise. The individual actor's primary objective in playing
PRINCEdown is to score as many points or at least to have as few
charged against him or her as possible. Consequently, players must fully
understand the scoring procedure as well as their role in the exercise.

Setting Up the Game

We will discuss how to set up the game assuming that you already have
a profile for the exercise. The PRINCEdown profile that follows is for
the family discussed in Chapter 2. Notice that it identifies issues, actors,
issue positions, power, and salience. This is similar to the information
used throughout the book. To understand fully PRINCEdown 2, you
might want to play through a few setups of the family example. However, PRINCEdown 2 is designed so that you can explore your own
political interests. An empty profile form appears at the end of this
chapter for you to use on the problem you are studying. If you wish to
play more than one cycle, make copies of the form. Once you have
mastered the rules of PRINCEdown 2 with the sample profile, you will
want to build the one germane to your particular interest.

Once you have selected a profile, decide which actor each of the individuals will play. If more than one student plays a particular actor,
those players must agree unanimously on any move their actor makes.
Each actor should receive salience chips of the appropriate color, as
indicated in the profile, as well as a supply of red power chips. Now
that each player has the appropriate number of chips, the next task is
to set up an issue board for each of the issues identified in the profile.
There follows a picture of what an issue board should look like. Copy
the number of boards you need — one for each issue — and place them
in a row so that players have easy access to them. Follow the pattern of
the issue board shown on page 150, making certain the squares of your
board are large enough to hold several chips. Your completed board
should be at least 10 inches by 4 inches. Also obtain sufficient red
(power) chips and separately colored chips for each actor. You should
obtain the smallest chips possible.

Now that you have the materials and necessary information, set up
the issue board by placing salience and power chips on the appropriate
spot. The P2P sheet will inform you of your starting issue positions
(IP's) by indicating a value ranging from +3 to –3 at the beginning of
the game for each of the issues that is being played. Your P2P sheet will
also tell you how important, or salient, each issue is to you. Salience
(SAL) is measured on a three-point scale ranging from 3 (extremely important) through 1 (of low importance). Your SAL on each issue deter-

PRINCEdown 2 Profile
Issue Area: The Family PRINCE

Issues:

1. Mother's right to bowl on Thursday nights.
2. Father's right to unlimited clothing expenditures.
3. Sister's desire to have her allowance increased from 10 to 15 cents (she is twelve years old).
4. Brother's freedom to stay out on weekday nights (he is a precocious ten-year-old).
5. A family visit to grandma's next week.

Actors (color)	#1			#2			#3			#4			#5		
	IP	P	S	IP	P	S	IP	P	S	IP	P	S	IP	P	S
1. Father (brown)	-3	2	3	+3	3	2	-2	3	3	-1	3	3	-3	1	1
2. Mother (blue)	+3	3	3	-2	1	2	-1	2	2	-3	2	2	+3	3	3
3. Sister (orange)	+1	1	1	+1	1	1	+3	1	3	-1	1	1	-2	1	1
4. Brother (white)	-1	1	2	+2	1	1	0	1	1	+3	2	3	-2	1	1
5. Grandma (yellow)	+3	2	1	-3	1	3	+3	1	1	-3	1	3	+3	3	3
6. (green)															

mines how many chips of your color to place in the appropriate square on the IP recording board. Use the number of chips indicated under SAL in the P2P sheet. In other words for each issue you take the correct number of chips, based on a salience of 1, 2, or 3, put them in a pile, and place them on the correct square of the IP recording board, depending on where your starting IP is in the +3 to –3 range. You will notice that some actors will start in agreement on some issues (that is, they will start with their markers in the same IP square). In other cases there will be substantial disagreement among actors.

Your P2P sheet will also inform you of your power (POW) on each issue. Power is a measure of the relative capacity of an actor either to make a given policy outcome occur or to prevent its occurrence. Power

ISSUE POSITION

Replica of an issue board

Issue # _____

_____

+3

+2

+1

O

-1

-2

-3

𝕻𝖗𝖎𝖓𝖈𝖊𝖉𝖔𝖜𝖓

is measured on a four-point scale ranging from 3 (extremely powerful) through 0 (not at all powerful). On each issue add the appropriate number of POW chips (red chips) designated in your P2P sheet to the pile of your SAL chips.

A Cycle

Each cycle has three distinct parts:

1. Bargaining session   (15 minutes)
2. Decision period   (5 minutes)
3. Announcement of moves   (Time necessary to implement decisions)

Bargaining session

During the bargaining part of the cycle you should discuss with other actors any moves you would like to see them make in their IP's. They in turn will discuss with you moves they would like to see you make. When you have decided what moves you actually will make, you must write them down on a slip of paper and turn it in at the end of this part of the move. All of the written instructions must be given to the referee, who will read the moves and decisions aloud and adjust the board accordingly. Note: No chips may be physically moved until the decision period. Remember the following:

1. No matter what oral agreements you make with other actors, only you can actually decide upon your moves by writing them down at the end of the bargaining session. You are in no way obligated to live up to any agreements you have made during the bargaining session. In turn, you must wait to see if other actors have lived up to their agreements with you.

2. You may move one square in either direction on the IP recording board on each issue during any one bargaining session. However, you cannot move across zero. If you start with a positive IP, you must stay somewhere in the positive range or at zero. The same holds true for IP's that are negative at the start of the game. If you start the game with a zero IP, you may move in either direction on that issue during the game.

3. The initial distribution of POW chips may not be altered in any way. When an issue is dropped from the game, all POW chips on that issue are removed.

4. If you wish to resolve or kill an issue, you can call a PRINCE-down in your written instructions during the decision period. One actor may call for only one PRINCEdown in any decision period. You may not call a PRINCEdown to resolve or kill an issue if your IP on that issue is zero.

5. The bargaining session may last no more than fifteen minutes. After that time, no talking among participants is permitted.

Decision period

After the bargaining period is over, a decision period of no more than five minutes takes place. During that time, each actor, without any further conversation with other actors, fills out the decision form appearing at the end of this chapter. Note that the form allows you to record changes in your issue positions on any issue and indicate what PRINCEdown (if any) you wish to call.

The referee will make the moves and conduct the PRINCEdown calculations in the order that he or she receives the decision forms. The decision period lasts no more than five minutes. If decision forms are not received from an actor, it is assumed the actor has made no decisions.

Announcement of moves

The last part of the exercise takes place in two stages. First, the referee will make the moves indicated on the decision forms. Each actor's written instructions will be read aloud and his or her chips adjusted on the issue board accordingly. No actor can move more than one space on a turn and none can go on the other side of zero from the starting point.

The referee will then indicate the PRINCEdown calls in the order in which they were submitted. Any PRINCEdowns on the first form are dealt with, then the PRINCEdowns on the next, and so on. If more than one form calls for a PRINCEdown on one issue, calculations are made just once. (Gains and losses from successful or unsuccessful PRINCEdowns differ according to whether one or more people call for a PRINCEdown. See the section on scoring.)

PRINCEdown. Resolving an issue and killing an issue are two sides of the same coin. To resolve an issue means to achieve a positive outcome. Whether the issue is to be resolved or killed depends upon the IP of the actor calling the PRINCEdown. If his IP is positive, the PRINCEdown is an attempt at resolving the issue; if it is negative, it is an attempt to kill it. In either case, the PRINCEdown is handled in the same manner. Once a PRINCEdown on a particular issue is announced, all actors, with the exception of the actor calling the PRINCEdown, may move their IP on the issue one square in either direction, but not across zero. Once this is completed, each actor multiplies his IP times his POW times his SAL on the issue.

These resulting scores are then totaled for all actors. If the total is greater than +30 (if the actor has a positive IP) or a bigger negative number than –30 (if the actor has a negative IP), the issue has been successfully PRINCEdowned. If the total is less, that is, closer to zero than +30 or –30, the PRINCEdown is unsuccessful. Successfully PRINCE-downed issues are dropped from the agenda of active issues. Issues on which a PRINCEdown is unsuccessful are not changed in any way. They may be the subject of future PRINCEdowns.

Chart 13-1 is an example of the calculations of a PRINCEdown. Suppose a PRINCEdown is called by the actor with white chips in a sample situation with three actors. The actor who called the PRINCE-down had a negative IP (–3 in this case), so he is trying to kill the issue. To kill the issue, the total must be a larger minus number than –30. Because the total is only –1, the PRINCEdown is unsuccessful. Thus the issue is retained on the agenda of active issues.

Scoring

If a call for a PRINCEdown is successful, points are assigned as follows: If the PRINCEdown was called by an individual actor, that actor receives 20 points. If more than one actor calls a PRINCEdown, each receives 10 points. These points are entered under "PRINCEdown successes" on the PRINCEdown 2 scoresheet.

Actors other than the actor who called the PRINCEdown lose points. This is calculated by determining the difference between the actor's IP and +3 if the issue is resolved, –3 if killed, and multiplying this number times the actor's SAL on the issue. This can be calculated on the PRINCEdown 2 scoresheet under "PRINCEdown losses." In the example shown in Chart 13-2 the actor has lost 10 points because the

CHART 13-1. Calculations of a PRINCEdown.

Actor	IP	X	POW	X	SAL	=	IP X POW X SAL
Blue	+3	X	2	X	3	=	+18
Yellow	+2	X	2	X	2	=	+8
White	-3	X	3	X	3	=	-27
Total							-1

CHART 13-2. Calculating a PRINCEdown loss.

IP Resolution	Actor's IP	Difference in IP	X	Actor's SAL	=	Loss
−3 (issue successfully killed)	+2	5	X	2	=	10

issue was successfully killed (−3 resolution). The difference between the actor's IP and the resolution was 5, and his SAL was 2.

If a PRINCEdown is unsuccessful, points are assigned as follows: If one actor calls the PRINCEdown, he or she loses 20 points. If more than one calls, each loses 10 points. Losing points are entered on the PRINCEdown 2 scoresheet under "PRINCEdown failures." Actors other than the actor who called the PRINCEdown each *receive* 10 points. These points are entered on the PRINCEdown 2 scoresheet under "PRINCEdown successes."

The end of the game occurs when all issues have been successfully PRINCEdowned and removed from the agenda. If the game must be ended before all the issues have been removed from the agenda, the winner is determined by the total score at the time the game is ended in the following manner: On the P2P scoresheet, total the columns labeled "PRINCEdown successes," "PRINCEdown losses," and "PRINCE-down failures" separately. Then, using the space provided on the scoresheet, subtract the totals from "PRINCEdown losses" and "PRINCEdown failures" from the total for "PRINCEdown successes." The result is the actor's final score. The actor with the highest score is the winner.

Constructing Your PRINCEdown 2 Profile

The play of the game clearly depends heavily on the values in the PRINCEdown 2 profile sheet. That sheet contains the information about the actors and issues necessary for the game to be played. Sample PRINCEdown 2 profiles follow. Using one or more of these, you can profitably play PRINCEdown.

However, you may wish to construct your own PRINCEdown 2 profiles for use in playing the game. This section will provide you with some guidelines for developing a profile. At a minimum, you must complete the following information to have a usable profile:

1. Identify the issues.

2. Identify the actors.
3. Assign values on IP, POW, and SAL.

At your option, you may develop the above information through a research paper. Or you may simply compose a short scenario to give a fuller explanation of the entries on the profile sheet. Or you may simply wish to fill in the PRINCEdown 2 Profile.

The procedures for identifying the issues, actors, and the values for issue position, power, and salience were given in Chapter 10. However, given the structure of PRINCEdown 2, there are a few additional rules that must be followed: First, try to design the profile so that each actor has about the same total salience chips on the board. There should be *no more than* eight SAL chips per actor when there are three issues, nine SAL chips per actor with four issues, and ten SAL chips per actor with five issues. Second, power may be distributed unevenly among the actors, as it is in the real world. However, avoid allowing one actor to be the *most* powerful on all issues. In addition, avoid having an actor with zero power on several issues. Beyond these two points, you should set up the game so that bargaining and changes *must* occur before an

PRINCEdown 2 Profile
Issue Area: Budgetary Difficulties in a Small College

Issues:

1. Change to the semester system from the quarter system.
2. Abolish standard letter grades.
3. Increase the budget for the student cafeteria.
4. Adoption of AAUP Standards on Tenure and Promotion.

Actors (color)	#1			#2			#3			#4		
	IP	P	S	IP	P	S	IP	P	S	IP	P	S
1. Administration (brown)	+3	2	1	-2	3	2	-3	3	2	-3	3	3
2. Faculty (blue)	+1	3	2	-3	2	3	+1	2	1	+3	3	3
3. Students (orange)	-3	3	2	+3	3	2	+3	2	3	+1	2	1

issue can be successfully PRINCEdowned. The sample P2P's are set up with values that promote bargaining. To insure that the game *is* a game, rather than a series of sudden successful PRINCEdowns in the first move, your values for IP, POW, and SAL on a particular issue when multiplied and totaled for all actors should not sum to more than + or –20. The lower the absolute total on an issue's profile, the more bargaining will be encouraged.

Analyzing Your PRINCEdown 2 Results

After playing the PRINCEdown 2 game, you are ready to begin to think about applying the things you have learned in the game to the "real world." This section merely suggests some of the kinds of questions you might think about and discuss.

1. *Why did the participants act as they did during the game? Did the rules of the game make others behave differently than you thought they might? If so, why? Could the particular political environments in which we find ourselves influence our behavior greatly?*
2. *Would you expect the actors that you and others were playing to act as you did?*
3. *How realistic is the game?*

This discussion can be aided by systematically dealing with factors operating and not operating in the model. We have provided below a checklist of questions to ask yourself:

1. What was the role of time and communications in the game and how is it different from the real world?

2. What was the role of personality and group dynamics factors among the participants and to what extent would it operate in the real world?

3. How realistic, in retrospect, was the PRINCEdown 2 profile you used? Are there starting values for IP, POW, or SAL that you think should have been different? Are there any actors who should have been included? Should any of the issues that were included have been left out?

4. To what extent were the rules of the game realistic with respect to your issue area? Do the values of IP, SAL, and POW change as they do in actual situations?

5. Do the dynamics of the bargaining session correspond to actual bargaining as you have studied it? Were promises kept more or less

frequently in the game as compared to actual politics? What factors govern the keeping or breaking of promises?

6. When a PRINCEdown is called, are issues resolved in the same way as in actual politics? Is it easier or harder to resolve issues? What changes could be made in the way the issues are resolved to make the game more realistic?

After dealing with the question of changes and the reality of the game, you are ready to explore the relevance of strategies in the game to strategies that might be possible in the real world. Identify the strategy followed by each player and the degree of success of those players. Would similar strategies produce success in the real world?

PRINCEdown 2 Decision Form

Name of the Actor _____   **Cycle** _____

Changes in IP

Issue #	*From*	*To*
_____	_____	_____
_____	_____	_____
_____	_____	_____
_____	_____	_____
_____	_____	_____

PRINCEdowns called.   (List the Issue # below if you wish to call a PRINCEdown.)

PRINCEdown 2 Scoresheet

1. PRINCEdown successes   2. PRINCEdown failures

    _____   _____

    _____   _____

    _____   _____

    _____   _____

    _____   _____

    _____   _____

    _____

    Total =   Total =

3. PRINCEdown losses

IP Resolution	Actor's IP	Difference in IP	×	Actor's SAL	=	Loss
_____	_____	_____		_____		_____
_____	_____	_____		_____		_____
_____	_____	_____		_____		_____
_____	_____	_____		_____		_____
_____	_____	_____				_____
				Total =		

4. Final score

       Success total (from 1)   _____

       Minus failure total (from 2)   _____

       Minus loss total (from 3)   _____

           Final score =   _____

PRINCEdown 2 Profile
Issue Area: _____

Issues:

1. _____
2. _____
3. _____
4. _____
5. _____

Actors	#1			#2			#3			#4			#5		
(color)	IP	P	S	IP	P	S	IP	P	S	IP	P	S	IP	P	S

1. _____
   ( )

2. _____
   ( )

3. _____
   ( )

4. _____
   ( )

5. _____
   ( )

6. _____
   ( )

Michael K. O'Leary
William D. Coplin
Gary Brey
Sharon Dyer

PROBE, A Computer Simulation Model for PRINCE Analysis

We hope you now feel, as we do, that the PRINCE political accounting system can help you understand and deal with many different types of political situations. But even as useful as it is, it obviously is a highly simplified model of political activity, leaving out many important elements. The reason we have made it so simple is that we expect you to do all the calculations by hand. Besides, simplification is a good thing in helping you understand the fundamentals of a subject. If you are interested in going beyond the simple calculations described in the preceding pages, you might want to get hold of a computer program called PROBE (which stands for Policy Research, OBservation, and Evaluation). PROBE is based on the same general principles as the system you have been reading about, but it has some interesting differences. For one thing, it lets you try out some ideas about how a group of political actors bargains and otherwise influences one another in trying to change issue positions. Besides that, it is set up so you can easily try one set of numbers to see what prediction it makes, then change some of the numbers (making different assumptions about the situation you are studying) and see how that changes the results.

Finally, because of the speed of the computer, you can include more actors and issues in your analysis and still get the calculations done by the time the late show goes on. However, don't count on using that speed to get a PRINCE paper done at the last minute. Computers can sense when you're really in a hurry, and this makes them so nervous that they inevitably blow a fuse or otherwise foul up. (The PROBE program is available from the authors, either as a Fortran program or as a program for the Hewlett-Packard HP65 pocket programmable calculator. Please write if you are interested.)

General Description of PROBE

PROBE provides a technique for making an estimated projection of what decision will be made by a selected political actor either to support or oppose a selected policy output. Like other forms of PRINCE analysis, the topic you apply this to may range from face-to-face situations to governmental actions, and the actor may be any individual or group capable of making an authoritative decision. Written into the program are a set of assumptions to the effect that actors consider the positions of other actors as the basis for determining their own positions on authoritative decisions. In other words, PROBE is based upon a branch of social science called "reference group theory" in sociology,[1] "interest group theory" in political science,[2] and "dissonance theory" in psychology.[3] PROBE can be employed to answer a variety of specific questions relating to the likely output of a policy process, including an evaluation of alternative strategies to shape that process. It can also be used as a tool to develop and test theoretical propositions concerning the policy process.

The following concepts are used in this chapter:

1. *Policy Output* (PO)—a potential decision (typically favored by some and opposed by others) that involves the allocation of some value by a decision maker.
2. *Output Actor* (OA)—a group or individual decision maker who is accepted as having the authority to allocate values, i.e., the authoritative decision maker.
3. *Reference Actor* (RA)—an actor who can influence the OA.
4. *Reference Output* (RO)—a potential decision, like the PO, that is of joint concern to an OA and an RA.
5. *Issue Position* (IP)—the stance by a given actor (OA or RA) of support for, opposition to, or neutrality toward either a policy output or reference output.

---

[1] Robert Merton, "Continuities in the Theory of Reference Groups and Social Structure," *Social Theory and Social Structure* (Glencoe, Ill.: Free Press, 1957).
[2] David Truman, *The Governmental Process* (New York: A. Knopf, 1951).
[3] Leon Festinger, *A Theory of Cognitive Dissonance* (Evanston, Ill.: Row, Petersen, 1957).

6. *Salience* (SAL)—the importance that a given actor attaches to a given PO or RO.
7. *Power* (POW)—the relative capacity possessed by a given actor to do one of two things: to affect the likelihood of a policy or reference output taking place or to have an effect on the relationship between a given output and its intended outcomes.
8. *Reference Weight* (RW)—the index indicating the direction and amount of influence a reference actor has on the position taken by the output actor on the policy output. The reference weight is determined according to one of three possible sets of decision rules by which PROBE calculates how an OA will respond to an RA. The three sets of decision rules are:

Interest aggregation (IA). The OA determines his issue position on the policy output by representing the interests of the reference actors according to their issue position, power, and salience solely on the policy output.

Consistency (CN). The OA determines his issue position on the policy output by agreeing on the PO with those reference actors who agree with him on its most salient reference outputs.

Cross-issue bargaining (CB). The output actor determines his issue position on the policy output by agreeing on the PO with those reference actors who have high power on those reference outputs on which the OA has high salience.

PROBE determines what issue position the output actor will take on the policy output by estimating the reference weight for each reference actor according to one of the decision rules as specified by the user and then combining them. The formulas for calculating these reference weights are on page 182–185.

Designing a PROBE Analysis

Now you have been given a general introduction to the PROBE program. The best way to gain an additional understanding of the simulation is to begin to design your own PROBE analysis of a political situation. This section lists the eight steps that comprise a PROBE analysis.

Step 1: Identify the Policy Output
You Wish to Study

A policy output (PO) is a decision affecting the allocation of values by an actor or group of actors that have the authority to make such a decision. Examples of policy outputs are a parent's establishing a child's bedtime, a school board's deciding to eliminate sex education from the school curriculum, the president's establishing wage-price controls, or a U.S. senator's vote to support the ratification of a treaty regulating the use of international airspace. The domain covered by a policy output can range from an intimate face-to-face situation to the entire world society and can involve actions that affect the distribution of any identifiable set of values. Most examples of policy making involve many policy outputs. Many of them are highly general; many are quite specific. All such PO's are susceptible to a PROBE analysis, but each must be analyzed separately.

Furthermore, as a tool of political analysis, PROBE is most effective when applied to a very specific policy output involving a few individuals or, at most, small groups of individuals. (However, this suggestion does not preclude analyzing the PO's of a large institution or group because one can select a representative member of the group to serve as an actor. It is also possible to combine individuals to form a group that may be counted as an actor.) For example, instead of attempting to analyze the policy output decision involving the United States government, it is more useful to analyze the decision involving the secretary of state, a pivotal U.S. senator, a cohesive interest group, or other individuals and groups involved in government.

The most interesting PO's to study are those that have some chance of occurring in the near future. Because a PROBE analysis may be used as a tool to determine the likely output of a selected actor in the policy process, a PROBE analysis only makes sense when applied to a PO that is supported by some actors and opposed by others.

Step 2: Identify the Output Actor

The output actor is the actor (or one of the actors) who has the authority to determine the policy output. Many PO's require the affirmative action of several actors; therefore, it is rarely correct to say that there exists only one output actor. For example, in voting on a bill, each member of the legislature is an OA. Any group or individual identifiable as an OA can be analyzed by means of a PROBE analysis. However, only one OA at a time can be analyzed. It follows from our discussion of selecting PO's that it makes for a more manageable analysis to

choose a relatively specific OA. It is more productive to study one official or one legislator than the whole government or an entire Congress.

It is frequently difficult to identify the OA. The problem lies essentially in the nature of authority, which is often difficult to locate in any
given context. However, the following guideline should provide the
basis for the necessary identification: *An actor is authoritative when he
is accorded the right to make a decision by those who feel an obligation to implement it, whether they agree with him or not.* In the
examples of policy outputs described above, the output actors were
respectively the parent, the school board, the president, and the senator. Once the specific policy output and its related domain are selected,
it is usually easier to identify the OA.

Step 3: Identify the Reference Actors

Once you have selected the policy output you wish to study, the next
step is to identify all of those actors who might influence the OA. We
call these actors reference actors. In determining the OA's issue position, the PROBE program takes into account the issue position, power,
and salience of these RA's, simulating the way an actual policymaker
consults with other individuals and groups.

The selection of RA's is a difficult task. Patterns of influence are not
always clear. Furthermore, in most cases a given OA can potentially
have an unlimited number of RA's in mind. To keep the PROBE program within manageable limits, we have placed an arbitrary limit of
nine as the maximum number of RA's you can employ in any one
analysis. To reach this limit, you may want to group actors that share
similar issue position, power, and salience values. Another rule of
thumb to follow is to exclude the OA and the RA from the analysis
if both of them have zero power or salience values on the PO or the
reference outputs that involve them.

Step 4: Choose the Proper Decision Rule
to Calculate RW's

There are three sets of decision rules to choose from, each representing
one way in which the output actor might react to the reference actor.
There are many possible factors that may determine which decision rule
will predominate. The following questions and concepts will help you
determine if the decision rule referred to applies.

Interest aggregation decision rule. Does the output actor perceive
the RA to be a constituent whom he or she must serve? If so, choose

the interest aggregation (IA) decision rule. Output actors frequently play the role of representing the interests of certain individuals and groups. For example, legislators generally keep in mind a set of actors and interests they seek to serve through legislative activities. Sometimes the IA relationship is formally established as a representative-constituent situation. In other cases, an OA will informally assume that he or she represents the interests of a particular RA in decisions. For example, a father may attempt to represent his children's interests in many of his policy outputs. In still other cases, OA's may tend to ignore their formal constituents even though they are supposed to be legally and morally bound to represent their interests. In spite of this, it is usually possible to determine when OA's perceive themselves to be representing the interests of an RA.

You should note that the IA decision rule need imply neither a paternalistic attitude on the part of the OA nor an inferior, subservient position on the part of the RA. A congressman may apply the IA rule to a constituent out of fear of losing that constituent's support at the next election. In an extreme case, a congressman may be so far "in the pocket" of a special interest group that he may actually feel inferior to the constituent toward whom he applies the IA rule. (In all instances, OA's are assumed to be acting in defense of their own interests. Consequently, the IA decision rule formula is automatically used by the computer to calculate the RW for the OA's on themselves, as an "anchor" to their starting issue position.)

Consistency decision rule. Frequently, the OA's will react to the pressure of the RA on the basis of whether or not the RA's positions on other outputs are in agreement with their positions. To cite an example, the Soviet Union's issue position on the PO of allowing emigration of Soviet Jews has led many U.S. senators to oppose pro-Soviet policies on trade qustions. Such relationships may also occur because the political setting of the two sets of actors is so different that the OA can only react to the RA in a consistency (CN) framework. This situation indeed characterized the first twenty years of U.S. relations with the People's Republic of China.

Cross-issue bargaining decision rule. Does the OA perceive the RA as a legitimate participant in some collective decision over which they both have authority? Are the RO's relatively specific and/or interdependent? If the answers to these questions is "yes" choose the cross-issue bargaining (CB) decision rule.

When the OA considers him or herself to be closely associated with a particular RA in some collective decision-making process, the OA, it is assumed, will cross-issue bargain with the RA if there is some institutionalized setting in which the bargaining can take place. A U.S. senator, for example, will frequently agree to support another U.S. senator on a legislative act if that senator, in turn, agrees to support him on another legislative act. To take another example, the president of the U.S. might cross-issue bargain with the top leadership of the Soviet Union if they have sufficient diplomatic channels through which to bargain, and if they can identify a set of issues that they feel are legitimately linked together.

Two points that may cause confusion to the beginner should be mentioned. The decision rule an output actor may apply to a given RA may change over time. For example, U.S. relations with the U.S.S.R. were characterized by the consistency decision rule twenty years ago, but are now characterized by the cross-issue bargaining rule. More significant is the fact that an OA may apply more than one rule toward a given RA during the same time period. A husband may use cross-issue bargaining with his wife on one issue, but look at her as one who's interest he should serve on another issue (IA).

Therefore, you will frequently find it difficult to apply the above rules when doing a PROBE analysis. You must make the best judgment possible and then run the program. If still uncertain, you may make different assumptions (changing the decision rule), rerun the program, and see if it makes any difference. The capacity to test the consequences of alternative assumptions is one of the advantages of a simulation program such as PROBE.

Step 5: Identify the Reference Outputs

If you have chosen the interest aggregation decision rule for a reference actor, you need not identify reference outputs. However, if you have chosen the consistency or cross-issue bargaining decision rules to represent the relationship between the output actor and any given reference actor, you will need to select the outputs that are of common concern to the output actor and each of the reference actors. You should select those RO's that are the most important to both the output actor and the reference actor. Usually, if the relationship between the OA and the RA is guided by the consistency decision rule, the kinds of RO's chosen will be relatively broad in nature. For example, if a U.S. senator were the OA and the Soviet Union were the RA, this would suggest selecting general Soviet or American policy decisions as the RO's. If the relationship between the OA and the RA is characterized by the cross-issue bargaining decision rule, the RO's are usually more narrow and technical than they would be if the consistency decision rule were operating between the OA and the RA. In a cross-issue bargaining situation, for example, a U.S. senator may agree to exchange his vote on one bill for another senator's support on another bill.

In choosing RO's you should pick those on which the OA and the RA have some salience and/or power. To be specific, you should *not* choose any RO for which both the OA and the RA have zero power or zero salience. You should also remember that you may only include a maximum of nineteen RO's in any PROBE analysis.

Step 6: Generate the Data

Once you have completed the first five steps, you are ready to collect the information you will need to do a PROBE analysis. In addition to the labels for outputs and actors, there are three types of information that you enter into PROBE: issue position, power, and salience. These terms are described throughout the book. Specifics on data collection appear in Chapter 10.

Step 7: Enter the Data onto Forms

On the next few pages we have included a series of forms to be used in recording the results of following the six steps so far outlined. You may use these for your own PROBE analysis. These forms will prepare you for completing Step 7 because they ask for the data in the same order as the PROBE program will ask for it. (See the sample PROBE run on pages 170–173.) The forms should be filled out as you go through the various steps described above. Each operation to be followed is indicated in the appropriate place on the chart. These operations and the chart to use to enter the information are indicated below.

Operation 1: Identify the policy output.   Enter its full name and a four-letter abbreviation in the place indicated on Chart 14-1.

Operation 2: Identify the output actor.   Enter his full name and a four-letter abbreviation in the place indicated in Chart 14-2.

Operation 3: Identify a maximum of nine reference actors.   Enter their full names and four-letter abbreviations in the place indicated in Chart 14-2. After completing this step, indicate the total number of actors at the top of Chart 14-2.

Operation 4: Identify the decision rules to calculate the reference weights for each actor. Enter the appropriate abbreviation next to each reference actor as indicated in Chart 14–2.

Operation 5: Select the appropriate reference outputs for each reference actor. Enter their full names and four-letter abbreviations in the place indicated in Chart 14–1.

Operation 6: Generate the data. Estimate the issue position, power, and salience values for the OA and the RA's. Remember that you will not have to gather data for all the actors on all the outputs. Keep the following guidelines in mind:

1. The OA must have IP, POW, and SAL values for the policy outputs and all the reference outputs.
2. Each RA must have values for the policy output.
3. RA's who affect the OA according to the IA decision rule will not have any data for any of the reference outputs.
4. RA's to whom the CN or CB decision rules apply will require data for one or more reference outputs that are of joint concern to the OA and the RA.

Operation 7: Enter the data in the IP, POW, and SAL matrices. After gathering your data, record IP on Chart 14–3, POW on Chart 14–4, and SAL on Chart 14–5. Label each chart with the four-letter actor and output abbreviations. Then enter the appropriate numbers in the squares of each chart.

You must enter something in each square corresponding to an actor and an output. If no IP, POW, or SAL value is necessary for a given square, enter the number 99, which will be read by the computer as an instruction to ignore that particular square. Remember also that if you have selected fewer than ten actors and twenty outputs, you will have some empty cells in your three matrices. These empty cells will correspond to the unlabeled rows and columns of the matrices. On page 205 we have included data matrices that you may use for your own PROBE analysis.

Step 8: Enter the Data in the PROBE Program

There are two ways to enter data in the PROBE program. One method involves the use of an interactive program in which the user sits at a computer console, calls up the program, and supplies the necessary information by typing it into the console. The other method is usually called "batch-processing"; the user keypunches a series of cards and uses a card reader to submit them, along with "system control cards," to the computer. You may wish to refer to pages 175–182 for instructions on keypunching the data cards, sample batch output, and sample batch data cards. The batch version, like the interactive version, will print out the estimated IP of the output actor on the policy output. Your instructor will inform you which method you are to use and provide you with specific instructions for using the computer.

After the interactive program prints out the estimated IP of the output actor on the policy output, it will ask you if you want to change any of the data you have entered. This is the opportunity for you to edit your data and to rerun the program to see what differences the new data produces. You can change any of the values you have entered for issue position, power, or salience, one at a time, prior to rerunning the program. This is a useful feature if you are unsure of some of your estimates and you want to see what difference it makes if you choose one estimate for a particular variable over another. The editing feature can also be used to examine the consequences of alternative political strategies you consider desirable or that you think one of the actors might implement. It can be used to see what would happen if, for instance, several actors increased their ability to affect outcomes of several outputs and, consequently, had their power values on several outputs raised.

To cite an example, the power of the Arab oil-producing nations to influence the stance of other nations (e.g., Japan) toward Israel rose dramatically when they finally imposed an oil boycott on the nations supporting Israel after years of conflict. A sample PROBE analysis devoted to the exploration of alternative political strategies concerning the behavior of France at the conference of oil-consuming nations is included on pages 193–201.

When using the interactive version of PROBE to inform the computer that you want to edit your data, you must type in the number of the actor whose data you wish to change, the number of the output for which you want to change the data, the matrix of the variable you wish to change (IP, POW, or SAL), and then the new value of the variable. However, it is slow to change values this way and then rerun the program. You should use this option only if you have just a few values to change. If you want to change many values and do a comparison run, it is more efficient to use the "batch-processing" version.

We have now presented all of the steps to follow in designing a PROBE analysis. In Figure 14–1 we have presented a flowchart summarizing these steps.

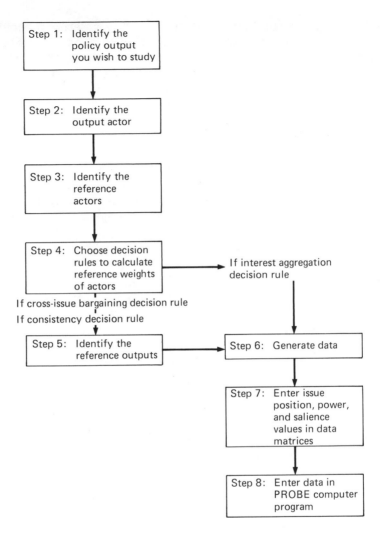

FIGURE 14-1. Flowchart for designing a PROBE analysis.

Sample PROBE Analysis

The following is an example of a PROBE analysis using the transformed data from the politics of a hypothetical family situation as described in Chapter 2, where a series of manual calculations similar to the PROBE program were described. We will go through the seven steps of a PROBE analysis very briefly, including the program as part of Step 8.

Step 1: Identify the policy output. The policy output we will be studying in this illustrative family situation is the right of the father to an unlimited clothing allowance.

Step 2: Identify the output actor. There is clearly one authoritative actor for this particular PO: the father.

Step 3: Identify the reference actors. In this illustration we will be content to list only four reference actors, the members of his immediate family. They are (1) the mother, (2) the daughter, (3) the son, and (4) his wife's mother, Grandma. His tailor, the cute young secretary at work, and many others might also have been included, but these four will suffice for our example.

Step 4: Identify the decision rules. The father and the mother are the two most closely interacting members of this group. The items they discuss include many specific and highly interrelated policy outputs in addition to the PO we have chosen to study. Therefore, we will select cross-issue bargaining as the decision rule determining how the mother will influence the father on the PO.

The father views his two children as clients whose interests he attempts to serve in the decisions he makes. Therefore, we will use the interest aggregation decision rule to determine the influence of the two children on the father.

The father and the grandmother have relatively formal "correct" dealings with one another. The father certainly does not see his mother-in-law as a client whose interests he represents; neither does the father have close and intense relations with her. Therefore, we will say that the consistency decision rule determines the relationship that the grandmother will have with the father.

Step 5: Select the reference outputs for each reference actor. In his dealings with the mother, the father is concerned with four outputs in addition to the policy output: (1) Mother's right to go bowling with the girls on Thursday night; (2) Brother's right to stay out at night as late as he wants to (now that he has reached the ripe old age of ten); (3) Sister's right to receive an increase in her allowance; and (4) the family's decision to visit Grandma on Sunday afternoon.

In their dealings with one another, Father and Grandma are concerned with two outputs in addition to the policy output: (1) Mother's right to go bowling on Thursday nights and (2) the decision to visit Grandma. (Note that there is some overlap in the reference outputs for two reference actors. This may or may not be the case in the analysis you perform. Also note that Brother and Sister, who are being dealt with according to the IA decision rule, have no reference outputs associated with them.)

Step 6: Estimate the data needed. For this illustration, this is the easiest part of all because the values are simply made up. Even so, it is similar to what you will be doing. Even if you perform a great deal of research to estimate your numbers, you will still be using them to summarize the political situation you are describing just as we are doing in this example.

Step 7: Enter the data on forms. On the following pages we have reproduced Charts 14-1 through 14-5, with the names and values associated with the hypothetical family entered according to the format you should follow in your own analysis.

Step 8: Enter the data in the PROBE program. On the pages following the charts we have reproduced a sample of the computer output of the interactive version of PROBE using the data from this family illustration. An example of the use of the editing feature has also been included in this PROBE run. (We assumed that if Grandma moved in with the family, the policy outcome would be affected. Because she is governed by the consistency decision rule, we used the editing option to change some of her issue position and salience values.) The form of the computer output is "system-specific" and consequently will vary with different computer systems. Your computer output may not be identical to this output. The hypothetical user in the family PROBE analysis has gone through the same eight steps you will go through in your own PROBE analysis. The underlining indicates information typed in by the user. Because the program has been initialized to run this data, you would be able to perform this analysis without entering the data yourself. We have entered the data, though, to show you the correct procedure.

Chart 14–1.

Total number of outputs ___5___

Step 1: Identify policy outputs

Output 1

SPND
(abbreviation)

Father gets clothing allowance
(full name)

Step 5: Identify reference outputs

Output 2

Bowl
(abbreviation)

Mother bowls
(full name)

Output 6

_____
(abbreviation)

_____
(full name)

Output 3

ALLW
(abbreviation)

Sister has allowance increase
(full name)

Output 7

_____
(abbreviation)

_____
(full name)

Output 4

FREE
(abbreviation)

Brother stays out late
(full name)

Output 8

_____
(abbreviation)

_____
(full name)

Output 5

VIST
(abbreviation)

Family visits Grandma
(full name)

Output 9

_____
(abbreviation)

_____
(full name)

Chart 14–2.

Total number of actors ___5___

Step 2: Identify output actor

Actor 1

FTHR
(abbreviation)

father
(full name)

Step 3: Identify reference actors

Actor 2

MTHR
(abbreviation)

mother
(full name)

Step 4: Choose decision rules
(IA, CN, CB)

___CB___

Actor 3

SSTR
(abbreviation)

sister
(full name)

___IA___

Actor 4

BTHR
(abbreviation)

brother
(full name)

___IA___

Actor 5

GNMA
(abbreviation)

grandma
(full name)

___CN___

ISSUE POSITION MATRIX   CHART 14-3
Policy and reference outputs

Output and reference actors

	SPND	BOWL	AIIW	FREE	VIST
FTHR	3	-3	-2	-1	-3
MTHR	-2	3	-1	-3	3
SSTR	1	99	99	99	99
BTHR	2	99	99	99	99
GNMA	-3	3	99	99	3

POWER MATRIX   CHART 14-4
Policy and reference outputs

Output and reference actors

	SPND	BOWL	ALLW	FREE	VIST
FTHR	3	2	3	3	1
MTHR	1	3	2	2	3
SSTR	1	99	99	99	99
BTHR	1	99	99	99	99
GNMA	1	2	99	99	3

SALIENCE MATRIX   CHART 14-5
Policy and reference outputs

Output and reference actors

	SPND	BOWL	AIIW	FREE	VIST
FTHR	3	3	1	3	1
MTHR	1	3	2	2	3
SSTR	1	99	99	99	99
BTHR	1	99	99	99	99
GNMA	3	1	99	99	3

SAMPLE PROBE OUTPUT

· ↑ C

·LOG
JOB 14 SYRACUSE UNIV 5Ø7A %1 TTY6
#1556,12
PASSWORD:
1 528   14–JUL–75   MON
   NOTE! EFFECTIVE THURSDAY, JULY 17, ALL TERMINALS WILL TALK
TO THE DECSYSTEM-1Ø VIA THE PDP-11. ALL SIGN-ONS MU ↑ 0

```
·EXEC PROBE
LOADING

PROBE 5K CORE
EXECUTION
```

THIS IS PROBE. DO YOU WANT TO SEE AN EXAMPLE
OF A PROBE ANALYSIS RUN?
ANSWER YES OR NO AND HIT THE CARRIAGE RETURN

NO

THIS IS PROBE. DURING THE COURSE OF EXECUTION
YOU WILL BE ASKED SEVERAL QUESTIONS. ANSWER EACH QUESTION
BY TYPING YES OR NO (FOLLOWED BY A CARRIAGE RETURN).
THE EXCEPTIONS TO THIS RULE ARE WHERE NUMERIC INFORMATION
IS REQUESTED.

DO YOU NEED DIRECTIONS ON THE USE OF PROBE?

YES

WHEN USING THE PDP-10 SYSTEM THERE ARE SEVERAL
THINGS YOU SHOULD KNOW. FIRST, IF YOU ENTER A NUMBER
WHERE AN ALPHABETIC CHARACTER WAS REQUIRED OR VICE VERSA
THE PROGRAM WILL TERMINATE. YOU WILL THEN RECEIVE A
MESSAGE ABOUT A FATAL I/0 ERROR. YOU MUST THEN RESTART
THE PROGRAM WITH THE EXE PROBE COMMAND.

IF AT ANY TIME YOU WANT TO TERMINATE THE EXECUTION OF THE
PROGRAM, SIMPLY HOLD DOWN THE KEY MARKED 'CTRL' AND
TYPE A 'C' TWICE. THIS WILL RESULT IN A C APPEARING AND
THE PROGRAM WILL END IMMEDIATELY .

THE PERIOD OR DOT (·) IS A MONITOR RESPONSE FROM THE
COMPUTER SIGNIFYING THAT THE SYSTEM IS READY TO ACCEPT
A COMMAND.

IF YOU TYPE A MISTAKE USE THE RUB OUT KEY (ON THE
RIGHT). HITTING RUB OUT WILL ERASE THE CHARACTER
IMMEDIATELY PRECEDING THE RUB OUT. IF YOU WANT TO ERASE THE
LAST THREE CHARACTERS YOU TYPED, YOU MUST HIT RUBOUT THREE
TIMES. WHEN YOU HIT THE CARRIAGE RETURN YOU HAVE INPUT THE
DATA YOU TYPED. THEREFORE, INSPECT EACH LINE BEFORE YOU HIT
THE RETURN.

WHEN YOUR JOB IS COMPLETED YOU WILL RECEIVE
A MESSAGE ABOUT CPU TIME AND A STATEMENT THAT SAYS
EXIT. TO SIGN OFF THE SYSTEM TYPE THE FOLLOWING:

KJOB/F   (AND HIT THE CARRIAGE RETURN)

IF YOU MAKE A MISTAKE AND BY CHANCE TYPE SOMETHING OTHER
THAN AN F THE SYSTEM WILL ASK YOU TO CONFIRM, RESPOND
WITH AN F. NEVER, REPEAT NEVER, TYPE A 'D' OR A 'K'
AFTER THE KJOB OR CONFIRM REQUEST.

WHEN USING THE PROBE PROGRAM YOU MUST ENTER EACH
REQUEST FOR INFORMATION BY LINE. IF YOU ARE ASKED FOR AN
ACTOR'S ISSUE POSITIONS YOUR RESPONSE MUST BE TO TYPE IN THAT
ACTOR'S ISSUE POSITION ON ALL ISSUES. E.G. IF THERE ARE
4 ISSUES, THE INPUT LINE FOR ACTOR X, WOULD CONTAIN
FOUR VALUES (WITH BLANKS BETWEEN) BEFORE TYPING A
CARRIAGE RETURN.

REMEMBER, FOR ANY OUTPUT THAT IS NOT RELEVANT TO
THE REFERENCE ACTOR, TYPE A 99 FOR ALL THREE MATRICES
IN THE SAME POSITION.

HOW MANY OUTPUTS IN THE SYSTEM? I.E. THE
POLICY OUTPUT PLUS ALL REFERENCE OUTPUTS.

5

YOU HAVE THE OPPORTUNITY TO ASSOCIATE A LABEL
WITH EACH OF YOUR OUTPUTS. ENTER EACH LABEL, I.E. NAME
AS IT IS REQUESTED. TYPE A FOUR CHARACTER
ABBREVIATION, THEN A BLANK AND THE FULL NAME.

OUTPUT 1

SPND

OUTPUT 2

BOWL

OUTPUT 3

ALLW

OUTPUT 4

FREE

OUTPUT 5

VIST

WHAT IS THE TOTAL NUMBER OF ACTORS IN THE SYSTEM?
THE OUTPUT ACTOR PLUS ALL REFERENCE ACTORS.

5

YOU CAN NAME YOUR ACTORS WITH A FOUR LETTER
ABBREVIATION. ENTER THE NAMES AS THEY ARE REQUESTED.

ACTOR 1

FTHR

ACTOR 2

MTHR

ACTOR 3

SSTR

ACTOR 4

BTHR

ACTOR 5

GNMA

ENTER AN ISSUE POSITION MATRIX IN THE MANNER
SPECIFIED IN THE DIRECTIONS.

ACTOR 1 FTHR

   3 -3 -2 -1 -3
ACTOR 2 MTHR

  -2 3 -1 -3 3
ACTOR 3 SSTR

   1 99 99 99 99
ACTOR 4 BTHR

   2 99 99 99 99
ACTOR 5 GNMA

  -3 3 99 99 3

ENTER AN ISSUE POSITION MATRIX IN THE MANNER
SPECIFIED IN THE DIRECTIONS.

ISSUE POSITION MATRIX

			SPND	BOWL	ALLW	FREE	VIST
ACTOR	1	FTHR	3.	-3.	-2.	-1.	-3.
ACTOR	2	MTHR	-2.	3.	-1.	-3.	3.
ACTOR	3	SSTR	1.	99.	99.	99.	99.
ACTOR	4	BTHR	2.	99.	99.	99.	99.
ACTOR	5	GNMA	-3.	3.	99.	99.	3.

ARE THESE DATA CORRECT?

YES

ENTER YOUR POWER MATRIX.

ACTOR   1 FTHR

  3 2 3 3 1

ACTOR   2 MTHR

  1 3 2 2 3

ACTOR   3 SSTR

  1 99 99 99 99

ACTOR   4 BTHR

  1 99 99 99 99

ACTOR   5 GNMA

  1 2 99 99 3

POWER MATRIX

			SPND	BOWL	ALLW	FREE	VIST
ACTOR	1	FTHR	3.	2.	3.	3.	1.
ACTOR	2	MTHR	1.	3.	2.	2.	3.
ACTOR	3	SSTR	1.	99.	99.	99.	99.
ACTOR	4	BTHR	1.	99.	99.	99.	99.
ACTOR	5	GNMA	1.	2.	99.	99.	3.

ARE THESE DATA CORRECT?

YES

ENTER YOUR SALIENCE MATRIX.

ACTOR   1 FTHR

  3 3 1 3 1

ACTOR 2 MTHR

  1 3 2 2 3

ACTOR   3 SSTR

  1 99 99 99 99

ACTOR   4 BTHR

  1 99 99 99 99

ACTOR   5 GNMA

  3 1 99 99 3

SALIENCE MATRIX

	SPND	BOWL	ALLW	FREE	VIST
ACTOR 1 FTHR	3.	3.	1.	3.	1.
ACTOR 2 MTHR	1.	3.	2.	2.	3.
ACTOR 3 SSTR	1.	99.	99.	99.	99.
ACTOR 4 BTHR	1.	99.	99.	99.	99.
ACTOR 5 GNMA	3.	1.	99.	99.	3.

ARE THESE DATA CORRECT?

YES

YOU MUST DEFINE THE DECISION RULE THAT OPERATES
BETWEEN THE OUTPUT ACTOR AND EACH OF THE REFERENCE ACTORS.
RESPOND WITH IA FOR INTEREST AGGREGATION, CN FOR
CONSISTENCY, AND CB FOR CROSS-ISSUE BARGAINING.

WHAT IS THE DECISION RULE BETWEEN THE OUTPUT ACTOR
AND ACTOR 2 MTHR

CB

WHAT IS THE DECISION RULE BETWEEN THE OUTPUT ACTOR
AND ACTOR 3 SSTR

IA

WHAT IS THE DECISION RULE BETWEEN THE OUTPUT ACTOR
AND ACTOR 4 BTHR

IA

WHAT IS THE DECISION RULE BETWEEN THE OUTPUT ACTOR
AND ACTOR 5 GNMA

CN

ON THE POLICY OUTPUT SPND

THE OUTPUT ACTOR'S ESTIMATED ISSUE POSITION IS: 2.

CONTRIBUTING TO THIS DECISION THE INFLUENCE OF EACH OF THE
OTHER ACTORS IS:

ACTOR	DECISION RULE	REFERENCE WEIGHT	STARTING ISSUE POSITION	POWER	SALIENCE
1 FTHR	IA	1.00	3.	3.	3.
2 MTHR	CB	0.51	-2.	1.	1.
3 SSTR	IA	0.11	1.	1.	1.

ACTOR	DECISION RULE	REFERENCE WEIGHT	STARTING ISSUE POSITION	POWER	SALIENCE
4 BTHR	IA	0.11	2.	1.	1.
5 GNMA	CN	−0.78	−3.	1.	3.

DO YOU WISH TO CHANGE ANY OF THE DATA AND RERUN THE PROGRAM?

YES

WHICH MATRIX DO YOU WANT TO REVISE?
USE IP TO INDICATE THE ISSUE POSITION, POW FOR POWER
AND SAL FOR SALIENCE.

IP

WHICH VALUE DO YOU WANT TO REPLACE?
SPECIFY THE NUMBER OF THE ACTOR.

2

AND THE NUMBER OF THE OUTPUT?

1

AND WHAT IS THE NEW VALUE?

−3

DO YOU WANT TO CHANGE ANOTHER VALUE?

YES

WHICH MATRIX DO YOU WANT TO REVISE?
USE IP TO INDICATE THE ISSUE POSITION, POW FOR POWER
AND SAL FOR SALIENCE.

IP

WHICH VALUE DO YOU WANT TO REPLACE?
SPECIFY THE NUMBER OF THE ACTOR.

5

AND THE NUMBER OF THE OUTPUT?

1

AND WHAT IS THE NEW VALUE?

0

DO YOU WANT TO CHANGE ANOTHER VALUE?

NO

THESE MATRICES ARE USED TO PRODUCE THE OUTPUT.

ISSUE POSITION MATRIX

	SPND	BOWL	ALLW	FREE	VIST
FTHR	3.	-3.	-2.	-1.	-3.
MTHR	-3.	3.	-1.	-3.	3.
SSTR	1.	99.	99.	99.	99.
BTHR	2.	99.	99.	99.	99.
GNMA	Ø.	3.	99.	99.	3.

POWER MATRIX

	SPND	BOWL	ALLW	FREE	VIST
FTHR	3.	2.	3.	3.	1.
MTHR	1.	3.	2.	2.	3.
SSTR	1.	99.	99.	99.	99.
BTHR	1.	99.	99.	99.	99.
GNMA	1.	2.	99.	99.	3.

SALIENCE MATRIX

	SPND	BOWL	ALLW	FREE	VIST
FTHR	3.	3.	1.	3.	1.
MTHR	1.	3.	2.	2.	3.
SSTR	1.	99.	99.	99.	99.
BTHR	1.	99.	99.	99.	99.
GNMA	3.	1.	99.	99.	3.

NOTE: 99. IS AN UNDEFINED POSITION.

ON THE POLICY OUTPUT   SPND

THE OUTPUT ACTOR'S ESTIMATED ISSUE POSITION IS: 1.

CONTRIBUTING TO THIS DECISION THE INFLUENCE OF EACH OF THE OTHER ACTORS IS:

ACTOR	DECISION RULE	REFERENCE WEIGHT	STARTING ISSUE POSITION	POWER	SALIENCE
1 FTHR	IA	1.ØØ	3.	3.	3.
2 MTHR	CB	Ø.51	-3.	1.	1.
3 SSTR	IA	Ø.11	1.	1.	1.
4 BTHR	IA	Ø.11	2.	1.	1.
5 GNMA	CN	-Ø.44	Ø.	1.	3.

DO YOU WISH TO CHANGE ANY OF THE DATA AND RERUN THE PROGRAM?

NO

THIS IS THE END OF PROBE ANALYSIS.

END OF EXECUTION
CPU TIME: 4.Ø2 ELAPSED TIME: 15:3Ø.53
EXIT

·KJOB/F
JOB 8, USER [1556,12] LOGGED OFF TTY! 1343 15–JUL–75
SAVED ALL FILES (295 BLOCKS)
RUNTIME 8.34 SEC

CHARGE: $1.29=$Ø.84(C)+$Ø.37(P)+$Ø.Ø8(K)
Y-T-D ACCOUNT USE: 24%

EQUATIONS FOR DECISION RULES

The PROBE analysis takes the form of using the data to generate the issue position of the output actor on the policy output according to three different decision rules. The three decision rules are (1) interest aggregation (IA); (2) consistency (CN); and (3) cross-issue bargaining (CB). Before describing the equations underlying each of the decision rules, we will describe some of the features shared by all three. The basic overarching assumption that all three decision rules employ is that the output actor will adopt an issue position that is a weighted average of the issue positions of all actors in the system, as it is defined by the data supplied by the user. The weighting is calculated according to one of the three decision rules explained below. Therefore, aggregating the weights generated by the reference weights of each reference actor, the estimated issue position of the output actor is calculated according to equation 1:

$$(1) \qquad ETx' = \frac{\displaystyle\sum_{i=1}^{n} (T_i' \times R_i')}{\displaystyle\sum_{i=1}^{n} R_i'} \qquad\qquad \left\{-3 \leqslant ETx' \leqslant +3\right\}$$

Where: ETx' = the estimated issue position of the output actor on the policy output.

n = the total number of actors (reference actors and the output actor) in the system.

T' = the issue position of each actor (reference actors and output actor) on the policy output.

R' = the reference weight of each actor (reference actors and output actor) on the policy output.

and i = the summation index indicating inclusion of values for T' and R' for all actors, 1 through n.

Note that the initial issue position of the output actor, with appropriate reference weight, is included in the calculation of the estimated issue position. This is because an output actor will consider his or her own position on the policy output along with the positions of the appropriate reference actors.

It is obvious that one critical variable in determining the output actor's estimated issue position is the reference weight of each of the actors. It is in the calculation of these reference weights, used to weight the issue positions of the actors, that the decision rules differ. We shall now describe the essentials of the formulas for calculating the reference weights under each decision rule.

Interest Aggregation Decision Rule

The first decision rule operates when the output actor will act so as to satisfy the dominant weight of interest of a reference actor with respect to the policy output. In this instance, interest is operationalized as the linear multiplicative function of power and salience on the policy output. The reference weight (Ry') for each reference actor is calculated according to equation 2:

$$(2) \qquad Ry' = \frac{Sy' \times Py'}{9} \qquad\qquad \left\{ 0 \leqslant Ry' \leqslant +1 \right\}$$

Where: Ry' = the reference weight, on the policy output, of the particular reference actor governed by the interest aggregation decision rule.

Sy' = the salience of the policy output for that particular reference actor.

Py' = the power of that particular reference actor with regard to the policy output.

and, the value 9 in the denominator is the product of the maximum possible values of S and P, used to normalize Ry' within the range 0 through $=1$.

Note that the reference weight of the output actor, used to weight his or her initial issue position, is calculated according to the interest aggregation decision rule.

Consistency Decision Rule

The second decision rule operates when the output actor is expected to take a position vis-à-vis a reference actor based upon the output actor's general political relationship with the reference actor. If the output actor enjoys general issue position agreement (small issue position difference across all outputs) with the reference actor, he or she will be pressured to agree with the reference actor on the policy output. If the OA has a large issue position difference across the outputs, he or she will be pressured to disagree with the reference actor. The pressure felt results in part from the issue position of each reference actor and the issue position and salience of the output actor on that output. The reference weight for each reference actor governed by the consistency decision rule is calculated according to equation 3 for each reference output:

If $Tx_i \times Ty_i$ is negative, (that is, the output actor and the reference actor have issue positions with differing signs), then:

$$(3a) \quad Ry' = \left(\frac{1}{m}\right) \sum_{i=1}^{m} \left[\left(\frac{|Tx_i - Ty_i|}{6} \times \frac{Sx_i}{3}\right) \times -1\right]$$

$$\left\{-1 \leqslant Ry' \leqslant 0\right\}$$

If $Tx_i \times Ty_i$ is zero or positive, (that is, the output and reference actors either have issue positions with the same sign or one has a zero issue position), then:

$$(3b) \quad Ry' = \left(\frac{1}{m}\right) \sum_{i=1}^{m} \left[\left(1 - \frac{|Tx_i - Ty_i|}{3}\right) \times \frac{Sx_i}{3}\right]$$

$$\left\{0 \leqslant Ry' \leqslant +1\right\}$$

Where: Ry' = the reference weight, on the policy output, of the particular reference actor governed by the consistency decision rule,

m = the number of outputs,

Tx = the issue position of the output actor on the output in question,

Ty = the issue position of the reference actor on the output in question,

Sx = the salience of the output in question, to the output actor,

i = the summation index indicating inclusion of values of Tx, Ty, and Sx, for all outputs from 1 through m,

and, the values in the denominator (6 and 3), are the maximum possible values or range of values appropriate to their numerators, used to normalize Ry' within a range of –1 through +1.

Note that the reference weight in this decision rule formula—unlike the reference weights calculated by the other two decision rule formulas—may take on a positive or a negative sign. (The reference weights of the other two decision rule formulas are always positive.) The operational meaning of this is that for the consistency decision rule, a given reference actor may work to move the output actor toward the issue position of the reference actor on the policy output (if it is positive) or away from the issue position of the reference actor on the policy output (if it is negative). For the other two decision rules, reference weights work only as varying pressures for agreement between the output actor and the reference actors.

Cross-Issue Bargaining Decision Rule

The third decision rule used in PROBE operates when an output actor is expected to maximize his or her utilities by supporting a reference actor when the reference actor has high power and the output actor has high salience. In short, the output actor will adopt his or her issue position on the policy output according to salience relative to the reference actor's power on each of the outputs in the system. The reference weight for the cross-issue bargaining decision rule is computed according to equation 4:

$$(4) \qquad Ry' = \left(\frac{1}{m}\right) \sum_{i=1}^{m} \left(\frac{Py_i \times Sx_i}{\max P_i \times \max Sx}\right) \qquad \{0 \leqslant Ry' \leqslant = 1\}$$

Where: Ry' = the reference weight, on the policy output, of the particular reference actor governed by the cross-issue bargaining decision rule,

m = the number of outputs,

Py = the power of the reference actor on the output in question,

Sx = the salience of the output actor on the output in question,

$\text{max}P$ = the maximum power score of any actor on the output in question,

$\text{max}Sx$ = the maximum salience of the output actor on all outputs in the system,

i = the summation index indicating inclusion of values of Py, Sx, and $\text{max}P$, for all outputs from 1 through m,

and, the product of $\text{max}P$ and $\text{max}Sx$ in the denominator is used to normalize Ry' within a range of 0 through +1.

Mathematical Notation for PROBE

x = output actor   A prime ($'$) used with x or y indicates a variable relating to the policy output only.

y = reference actor   The absence of the prime indicates a variable relating to any output.

T = issue position (any actor).

ETx' = the estimated issue position of the output actor on the policy output.

Tx' = the initial issue position of the output actor on the policy output.

Tx = the issue position of the output actor on an output.

Ty' = the issue position of a reference actor on the policy output.

Ty = the issue position of a reference actor on an output.

R = reference weight (any actor).

Rx' = the reference weight of the output actor.

Ry' = the reference weight of a reference actor.

S = salience (any actor).

Sx' = the salience of the policy output for the output actor.

Sx = the salience of an output for the output actor.

Sy' = the salience of the policy output for a reference actor.

Sy = the salience of an output for a reference actor.

P = power (any actor).

Px' = the power of the output actor on the policy output.

Px = the power of the output actor on an output.

Py' = the power of a reference actor on the policy output.

Py = the power of a reference actor on an output.

n = the number of actors.

m = the number of outputs.

$maxP$ = the maximum power score of any actor on the output in question.

$maxSx$ = the maximum salience of the output actor on all outputs in the system.

i = the summation index indicating the range of relevant values to be included in a summation operation.

USING THE "BATCH-PROCESSING" VERSION OF PROBE

If you do not have a conversational computer available (i.e., in which the user interacts directly with the computer through some type of terminal), you will use the "batch-processing" version of PROBE, in which the data is entered into the program by means of punched cards. Even if a conversational system is available, the experienced PROBE user may want to use the batch version to run a number of PROBE analyses without having to spend the time at a terminal. There is general correspondence between the data entered into the interactive version and the batch version. However, the data is put into a slightly different organization (or format).

Because there are many differences between computer systems and computer installations, we cannot give you instructions for running the

PROBE program here. Your instructor will give you directions for running PROBE at your computer center. Instructions should include key-punching some special cards (*Job Control Language* cards) to instruct the computer to run the PROBE program. In addition to these JCL cards, you will punch your own data cards.

The cards you must punch are described in the sequence in which they must be submitted to the program. If you submit a run that does not follow this sequence, then PROBE cannot process the run correctly. The data you input is checked for errors by PROBE and any data that is out of bounds (i.e., numbers that are not included in the IP, POW, or SAL scales) will be reported to you. Cards that are out of sequence will probably result in a computer error message that will be unintelligible to you. If this happens, the first thing you should check is the sequence of your cards. (Figure 14-2 shows the proper sequence of cards for three consecutive PROBE analyses. The first two analyses involve the same sets of actors and outputs; the third analysis involves different sets of actors and outputs.)

The batch version is programmed to do as many PROBE analyses of as many data sets as you wish with one pass through the card reader. The repetition of analyses is controlled by the title card and is explained below. Each analysis requires a set of data cards. However, the cards included in this set will vary depending on the type of analysis. These differences will be noted below.

Title card.   The title card has two functions: (1) to provide descriptive information about the run and (2) to control the consecutive execution of runs. All eighty columns of this card are available to you to label the PROBE analysis. Punch your run title starting in column 1 and continue as though you are typing a sentence. Remember that the title cannot exceed eighty columns. If you want to perform another analysis using the same actors and outputs as in the previous analysis but with some changes in the data, the first four columns of the title card for the second analysis must contain the word SAME. Columns 5–80 are available for punching any other information you want in the title. If the title card contains the control word SAME for an analysis, do *not* include the number of actors/number of outputs card, the output label cards, or the actor/decision rule cards. Only the issue position cards, power cards, and salience cards are included in a SAME analysis.

Number of actors/number of outputs card.   In columns 1–2 punch the total number of actors to be included in the analysis (i.e., the output actor plus all of the reference actors). Leave column 1 blank if there are fewer than ten actors. (For example, if there are five actors, punch 5 in column 2.) Leave column 3 blank. In columns 4–5 punch the total number of outputs (i.e., the policy output plus all of the reference outputs).

Output label cards. You must punch one of these cards for each output in the analysis. When you have finished punching these cards, check to make certain that the number of cards equals the number of outputs in the analysis. In columns 1–4 of each card punch a four-letter abbreviation for an output, starting with the policy output and continuing with each reference output until all the outputs are labeled. These cards must be punched and entered into the program in the same order in which you will be entering the data. (In our sample analysis of the family situation, there are five outputs so we punched five output label cards.)

Actor/decision rule cards. You must punch one of these cards for each actor in the analysis. When you have finished punching these cards, check to make certain that the number of cards equals the number of actors. In columns 1–4 of the first actor/decision rule card, punch a four-letter abbreviation for the output actor and leave the rest of the card blank. In columns 1–4 of each subsequent card, punch a four-letter abbreviation for a reference actor. Leave column 5 blank. In columns 6–7 punch the two-letter abbreviation of the decision rule operating between the output actor and that reference actor (IA for interest aggregation, CN for consistency, and CB for cross-issue bargaining). These cards must be punched and entered into the program in the same order in which you will be entering the data.

Issue position cards. In columns 2–3 of the first issue position card of this set enter the issue position (IP) of the output actor on the policy output. In column 2 punch a minus sign if the issue position is negative. If it is positive, leave column 2 blank. Never punch a plus sign for a positive issue position.

In column 3 punch the issue position number. In columns 5–6 punch the IP of the output actor on the second output (i.e., the first reference output) using the same procedure as with the policy output. Continue in the same way for all the IP's of all of the reference outputs for the output actor.

In the second card of this set punch the IP for the first reference actor on the policy output in columns 2–3 in the same way as you did for the output actor. Continue on in columns 5–6, 8–9, etc., punching the IP's for the first reference actor on each reference output. (Leave columns 1, 4, 7, etc. blank.) You will not, of course, have actual data for every reference actor for every reference output. In every case where you do not have data, punch a 99 in the columns allotted for an issue position in that particular field. The computer will read this number as an instruction to ignore that particular data.

If you have the maximum number of outputs (20), the last issue position will be punched in columns 59-60. You will always end a card in the column that is the product of 3 times the number of outputs punched on the number of actors/number of outputs card. (In our sample run there are five outputs so we punched the last issue position in columns 14-15.) This formula also holds for checking the punching of power and salience cards.

Continue punching the IP's for each reference actor, starting a new card for each one. You will need one of these IP cards for each actor you are including in your PROBE analysis. These cards must be punched in the same order as the actor/decision rule cards so that the correct values will be associated with each actor.

Power cards.   Enter the power value of the output actor on each output in the last column of each three-column field allotted for a power value (i.e., in column 3 of the first three-column field, in column 6 of the second such field, etc.). Continue punching this card until you have assigned power values for the output actor on all of the outputs.

Continue in the same way with a separate card for each reference actor. For reference actors for whom you have no data for a particular reference output punch a 99 in the last two columns of that three-column field as an instruction to the computer to ignore that particular data. If you have the maximum number of outputs (20), the last column punched will be column 60. (In the sample batch run there are five outputs so the punching ends in column 15.)

Salience cards.   Finally, punch in the salience scores for the output actor and all of the reference actors, following exactly the same procedure as in punching the power cards. Make certain that you have punched these cards in the same order as the actor/decision rule cards so that the correct data will be entered for each actor.

Finish card.   The last card of your data deck must be a finish card. If you are doing several PROBE analyses at once, place this card at the end of the last set of data you want analyzed. This card tells PROBE that it has completed all of the analyses you want. The finish card is punched as follows: in columns 1-6 punch the letters FINISH.

Figure 14-2 is a schematic representation of the sequencing of a card deck that would be used to perform three consecutive PROBE analyses.

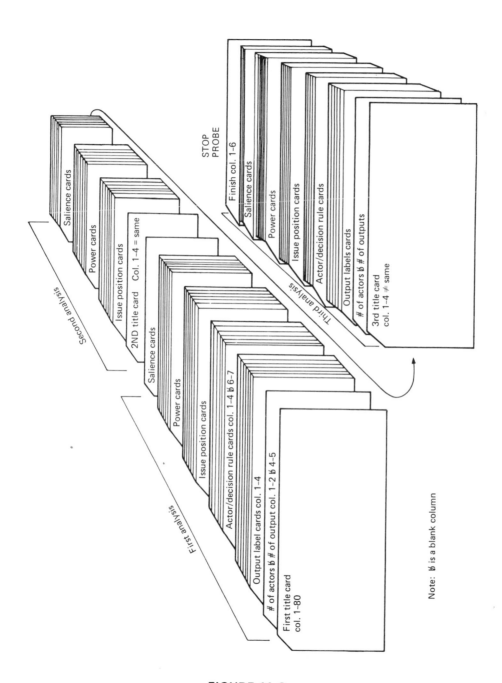

FIGURE 14-2.

The first two analyses concern the same actors and outputs but the third has a different set of actors and outputs. (Pay special attention to the location of the SAME and FINISH cards in this deck.) Following Figure 14-2 is the set of cards used in the batch version of the family politics situation. (To conserve space, we have only reproduced the relevant portion of each card.) Following that is a reproduction of the computer output of this PROBE analysis.

FAMILY POLITICS EXERCISE

THE FOLLOWING IS A LIST OF THE RUN PARAMETERS.

THE NUMBER OF OUTPUTS SPECIFIED IS: 5

THE NUMBER OF ACTORS SPECIFIED IS: 5

THE DECISION RULE BETWEEN THE OUTPUT ACTOR AND REFERENCE ACTOR MTHR IS: CB

THE DECISION RULE BETWEEN THE OUTPUT ACTOR AND REFERENCE ACTOR SSTR IS: IA

THE DECISION RULE BETWEEN THE OUTPUT ACTOR AND REFERENCE ACTOR BTHR IS: IA

THE DECISION RULE BETWEEN THE OUTPUT ACTOR AND REFERENCE ACTOR GNMA IS: CN

THESE MATRICES ARE USED TO PRODUCE THE OUTPUT.

ISSUE POSITION MATRIX

	SPND	BOWL	ALLW	FREE	VIST
FTHR	3.	-3.	-2.	-1.	-3.
MTHR	-2.	3.	-1.	-3.	3.
SSTR	1.	99.	99.	99.	99.
BTHR	2.	99.	99.	99.	99.
GNMA	-3.	3.	99.	99.	3.

POWER MATRIX

	SPND	BOWL	ALLW	FREE	VIST
FTHR	3.	2.	3.	3.	1.
MTHR	1.	3.	2.	2.	3.
SSTR	1.	99.	99.	99.	99.
BTHR	1.	99.	99.	99.	99.
GNMA	1.	2.	99.	99.	3.

```
              SALIENCE MATRIX
         SPND  BOWL  ALLW  FREE  VIST
FTHR     3.    3.    1.    3.    1.
MTHR     1.    3.    2.    2.    3.
SSTR     1.    99.   99.   99.   99.
BTHR     1.    99.   99.   99.   99.
GNMA     3.    1.    99.   99.   3.
```

NOTE: 99. IS AN UNDEFINED POSITION.

ON THE POLICY OUTPUT SPND

THE OUTPUT ACTOR'S ESTIMATED ISSUE POSITION IS: 2.

CONTRIBUTING TO THIS DECISION THE INFLUENCE OF EACH OF THE
    OTHER ACTORS IS:

ACTOR	DECISION RULE	REFERENCE WEIGHT	STARTING ISSUE POSITION	POWER	SALIENCE
1 FTHR	IA	1.00	3.	3.	3.
2 MTHR	CB	0.51	-2.	1.	1.
3 SSTR	IA	0.11	1.	1.	1.
4 BTHR	IA	0.11	2.	1.	1.
5 GNMA	CN	-0.78	-3.	1.	3.

FINISH
****

THIS IS THE END OF PROBE ANALYSIS.

FRANCE AND OIL CONSUMER COHESION—AN OUTLINE
OF THE STEPS IN A PROBE ANALYSIS

To assist you in learning the steps in a PROBE analysis, we have re-
printed a paper written by an undergraduate. The paper was written
expressly for the purpose of exploring alternative political strategies to
be used to persuade France to sign a communiqué. Therefore, it provides an excellent illustration of the possible uses of Western cooperation regarding energy of the editing option. (Note that although the
paper was written back in early 1974, it accurately forecasts France's
moderation on energy issues.)

Chart 14-6.

Total number of outputs _____5_____

Step 1: Identify policy outputs

Output 1

SIGN
(abbreviation)

France signs
Communique
(full name)

Step 5: Identify reference outputs

Output 2
M BFR
(abbreviation)

U.S. withdraws
troops from Europe
(full name)

Output 6
_ _ _ _ _ _ _
(abbreviation)

_ _ _ _ _ _
(full name)

Output 3
ISRA
(abbreviation)

Israel withdraws
troops
(full name)

Output 7
_ _ _ _ _ _ _
(abbrevation)

_ _ _ _ _ _
(full name)

Output 4
ARMS
(abbreviation)

France sells
arms to Arabs
(full name)

Output 8
_ _ _ _ _ _ _
(abbreviation)

_ _ _ _ _ _
(full name)

Output 5
EURO
(abbreviation)

Eur. states
form United Europe
(full name)

Output 9
_ _ _ _ _ _ _
(abbreviation)

_ _ _ _ _ _
(full name)

During the Arab oil boycott in February 1974, the leading oil-consuming nations met in Washington, D.C., to discuss the practicality of oil policy coordination and cooperation. All of the participants except France signed the final communiqué, which proposed various steps for joint action. The steps for performing a PROBE analysis of the French issue position with respect to signing the final communiqué in full are outlined below.

Step 1: Identify the policy output. The policy output has already been identified as France's signing the communiqué in full. However, because a policy output must be stated in terms of a specific outcome, the policy output is stated more formally as "France will sign the final communiqué in full."

Step 2: Identify the output actor. The other members of the conference recognize that France has the authority to decide whether or not she will sign the communiqué in full. So France is readily identified as the output actor.

Chart 14-7.

Total number of actors _____6_____

Step 2: Identify output actor

Actor 1

_F N C E_ _ _   _France_
(abbreviation)   (full name)

Step 3: Identify reference actors   *Step 4: Choose decision rules*
(IA, CN, CB)

Actor 2 *multinational*
_M N C S_ _   *oil corporations*   _____I A_____
(abbreviation)   (full name)

Actor 3
_W G E R._ _   *West Germany*   _____C B_____
(abbreviation)   (full name)

Actor 4
_U S A_ _ _   *United States*   _____C N_____
(abbreviation)   (full name)

Actor 5
_U N K M_ _   *United Kingdom*   _____C B_____
(abbreviation)   (full name)

Actor 6 *Arab*
_A R A B_ _   *oil-producing states*   _____C B_____
(abbreviation)   (full name)

 Step 3: Identify the reference actors. As the host nation and principal instigator of the conference, the U.S.A. must be considered as one reference actor. France's neighbors, West Germany and the United Kingdom, were largely dependent upon the Arab oil-producing nations for their oil fuel supply, as was France. Through the mechanisms of the Common Market they had some ability to influence France's decision, so they were counted as reference actors.

 The Arab oil-producing nations also had the ability to affect France's decision to sign the communiqué because they controlled the oil supply. If France sided with the oil-consuming nations against the Arab states, then the Arabs might continue the boycott as a reprisal. On the other hand, if France refused to sign, they might treat France more leniently and increase the oil supplies to France.

 The multinational oil corporations (MNCS) were included in this analysis as reference actors because they could potentially affect the flow of oil supplies to France. In turn, the formation of a bloc of oil-consuming nations, such as the one proposed at the conference, could affect the oil market, particularly if they refused to buy oil at the inflated prices the corporations were charging.

Step 4: Identify the decision rules. The multinational oil companies (especially those with offices in France) are only influencing France on the policy output—the decision to sign the communiqué. Furthermore, the oil companies are considered to be clients of France so the IA decision rule holds for this reference actor, particularly because France is not subordinate to the oil companies in this matter.

West Germany and the United Kingdom have close interactions with France, particularly through the Common Market decisions in which all participate. France also acknowledges that they possess status equal to her own, so the CB decision rule was selected for these reference actors. The oil-producing Arab nations are also accorded equal status by France and interact with France on economic issues. For these reasons, the CB decision rule was also selected for them.

Based upon the answers to the questions for choosing decision rules, the CN decision rule is appropriate for the U.S. France and the U.S. acknowledge each other as independent equals. However, there is conflict between them because France considers herself the leader of Europe and believes that the U.S. has usurped her role. The hostility between the two nations over this matter has overflowed into other areas. The U.S. government, for instance, refused to heed the advice of the French, who had fought in Indochina, while the U.S. was fighting in Vietnam. The U.S. resented the interference of the French, who, in turn, resented being ignored by the U.S. The hostility generated by this "positive feedback" system is not the principal determinant of U.S. relations with France. Consequently, the CN decision rule was selected for the U.S.

Step 5: Select the reference outputs. Because the IA decision rule was selected for the oil companies, no reference outputs have been identified for them. The sale of French arms to the Arab states is of concern to France and the Arab states, of course. The U.S. is a reference actor in this instance because of its interests in preventing war between Israel and the Arab states. Stated in terms of a specific outcome, this reference output is, "France sells arms to the Arab states."

For the reason cited above, the U.S. is also a reference actor in the decision of Israel to withdraw from the Arab lands captured since the 1967 war (i.e., Israel withdraws troops to pre-1967 boundaries). Naturally, the Arab states are counted as a reference actor because they intensely desire this outcome.

The reference outputs "The U.S. agrees to a mutual balanced forces reduction in Europe" and "European nations unite to form one state" are of concern to the U.S., the United Kingdom, and West Germany. France, the output actor, is of course considered to be involved in all of the reference outputs. A completed chart of outputs follows later in the paper.

Step 6: Generate the data. The *New York Times* was one data source used for this paper. Many of the necessary number values were obtained through a content analysis of articles concerned with the oil conference. To reproduce all of the quotes used to assign the IP, POW, and SAL values for the actors on their respective outputs would require too much space, so only a few examples are given below:

1. W. Germany and the United Kingdom were assigned a +2 issue position on the policy output on the strength of the following February 13 quote, "West German, British, Dutch, and Belgium spokesmen all publicly rebuked the French for trying to prevent the inclusion of provisions in the communiqué that would move the consuming nations toward a subsequent meeting to control oil prices and assure a stable oil supply."

2. On the matter of Israeli withdrawal, the U.S.A. was assigned a power value of 3, partly due to a remark made by a German official reported in the February 13 *Times*: "Mr. Schmidt said today that only the United States had been able to bring about an armistice in the Middle East and only the United States had the power and influence to maintain that armistice and bring about a political settlement."

3. The oil MNC's were assigned a −2 issue position on the policy output due to Exxon's Chairman J.K. Jamison's (February 17) opposition to "creation of a bargaining bloc of oil-consuming nations."

Values not derived from the *Times* were obtained by surveying two of my professors, identified below by the letters A and B, before conducting my PROBE computer analysis. Their estimates are given in Charts 14–8 through 14–10. The parentheses indicate data already obtained from the *Times* or cells for which data was not necessary (99). (Note: To obtain these results, the student used the questionnaire reproduced at the end of Chapter 10.)

Step 7: Enter the data in the matrices. The data supplied by my

CHART 14-8. Professors' estimates for issue position of actors.

		Sign	MBFR	ISRA	ARMS	EURO
FNCE	A	-3	+2	+3	+3	-1
	B	-3	+2	+3	+3	-1
MNCS	A	-1	(99)	(99)	(99)	(99)
	B	-3	(99)	(99)	(99)	(99)
WGER	A	(2)	-3	(99)	(99)	+3
	B	(2)	-3	(99)	(99)	+2
USA	A	+3	0	-1	-2	+3
	B	+3	+1	-3	-2	+1
UNKM	A	+2	-2	(99)	(99)	+2
	B	+2	-1	(99)	(99)	+2
ARAB	A	-3	(99)	+3	+3	(99)
	B	-3	(99)	+3	+3	(99)

CHART 14-9. Professors' estimates for power of actors.

		Sign	MBFR	ISRA	ARMS	EURO
FNCE	A	+3	+2	+1	+3	+1
	B	+3	+1	+1	+3	+1
MNCS	A	+2	(99)	(99)	(99)	(99)
	B	+1	(99)	(99)	(99)	(99)
WGER	A	+2	+3	(99)	(99)	+3
	B	+2	+3	(99)	(99)	+2
USA	A	+2	0	(2)	+2	+2
	B	+1	+1	(2)	+1	+2
UNKM	A	+1	+1	(99)	(99)	+2
	B	+2	+2	(99)	(99)	+1
ARAB	A	+3	(99)	+3	+3	(99)
	B	+3	(99)	+3	+3	(99)

professors was averaged to obtain a single estimate for each variable. This data for issue position, power, and salience, along with the data from the *Times*, was recorded in Charts 14–11 through 14–13.

Step 8: Enter the data in the PROBE program. The data in Charts 14–11 through 14–13 was then entered into the computer console as specified by the PROBE directions. The data matrices and the reference weights have been included in this paper.

As the original PROBE analysis print-out shows, the data I have

CHART 14–10. Professors' estimates for salience of actors.

		Sign	MBFR	ISRA	ARMS	EURO
FNCE	A	+3	+3	+1	+1	+3
	B	+2	+1	+2	+2	+3
MNCS	A	+3	(99)	(99)	(99)	(99)
	B	+3	(99)	(99)	(99)	(99)
WGER	A	+3	+3	(99)	(99)	+3
	B	+3	+3	(99)	(99)	+3
USA	A	+3	+3	+3	+2	+1
	B	+3	+2	+3	+2	+1
UNKM	A	+2	+1	(99)	(99)	+3
	B	+2	+2	(99)	(99)	+3
ARAB	A	+3	(99)	+3	+3	(99)
	B	+3	(99)	+3	+2	(99)

entered predicts that France will be opposed to the agreement, as indicated by its negative issue position. This is, of course, consistent with the stand France actually took. Interestingly enough, in this analysis France has a rather moderate negative issue position. If this analysis is correct, it would suggest that even though France is now sharply opposed to agreement with other Western countries on oil policy, there is pressure for her to modify her position. Perhaps over the long run we can expect that France will become less adamant and may even agree to some limited cooperation in the future.

Using the Editing Capability to Try
Different Strategies

I tried several different strategies to see if it would be possible to move France to become positive on signing the communiqué. First, I tried to make the U.S. move more sharply in disagreement with France to try to coerce her into agreement. But this had no effect, or, in some cases, made France even more opposed to signing.

The one possible strategy that might work had two parts to it. The first part would be to get both the United Kingdom and Germany to move to a more positive issue position. I would try to develop the strongest argument I could about the dangers of not working together and showing as much solidarity as possible in the face of a united OPEC group. The second part, which would probably be much more difficult, would be to get the Arabs to reduce their salience regarding the agree-

ISSUE POSITION MATRIX   CHART 14–11.
Policy and reference outputs

Output and reference actors

	SIGN	MBFR	ISRA	ARMS	EURO
FNCE	-3	2	3	3	-1
MNCS	-2	99	99	99	99
WGER	2	-3	99	99	2
USA	3	-1	-2	-2	2
UNKM	2	-2	99	99	2
ARAB	-3	99	3	-3	99

POWER MATRIX   CHART 14–12.
Policy and reference outputs

Output and reference actors

	SIGN	MBFR	ISRA	ARMS	EURO
FNCE	3	1	1	3	2
MNCS	2	99	99	99	99
WGER	2	2	99	99	2
USA	2	3	3	2	2
UNKM	2	2	99	99	2
ARAB	3	99	2	3	99

SALIENCE MATRIX   CHART 14–13.
Policy and reference outputs

Output and reference actors

	SIGN	MBFR	ISRA	ARMS	EURO
FNCE	3	2	2	2	3
MNCS	3	99	99	99	99
WGER	2	3	99	99	3
USA	3	2	3	2	1
UNKM	2	2	99	99	3
ARAB	3	99	3	3	99

ment, and also not allocate as much of their resource power to that issue. I would point out to them that we were not being hostile, just trying to reach some agreement so we could have stable negotiations between the producers and consumers of oil. I would have our ambassadors say that although we understand they would never come to agree with France signing the communiqué, they probably would be serving their own best long-run interests if they concerned themselves with development and other issues rather than this communiqué. The reason for picking the U.K., Germany, and the Arabs is because of reference weights. They have very high RW's on France.

To see what would happen under this strategy, I reran the data, changing the IP of the United Kingdom to +3 and changing the SAL and POW of the Arabs to 2 (from the previous 3). The results are shown in the edited PROBE run, which demonstrates that this does change France's IP. It has moved from a –1 to a 0. This means that accomplishing the things stated in the previous paragraphs would tend to make France even less negative than it is already. In the long-run it might even be possible to induce some limited cooperation between France and the U.S.

I realize that the next step should be to do PROBE analyses for changing the U.K., Germany, and the Arabs. However, because this paper is only 15% of my grade, we will have to save that analysis for another time.

ORIGINAL PROBE ANALYSIS

ISSUE POSITION MATRIX

		SIGN	MBFR	ISRA	ARMS	EURO
ACTOR 1	FNCE	-3.	2.	3.	3.	-1.
ACTOR 2	MNCS	-2.	99.	99.	99.	99.
ACTOR 3	WGER	2.	-3.	99.	99.	2.
ACTOR 4	USA	3.	-1.	-2.	-2.	2.
ACTOR 5	UNKM	2.	-2.	99.	99.	99.
ACTOR 6	ARAB	-3.	99.	3.	-3.	99.

POWER MATRIX

		SIGN	MBFR	ISRA	ARMS	EURO
ACTOR 1	FNCE	3.	1.	1.	3.	2.
ACTOR 2	MNCS	2.	99.	99.	99.	99.
ACTOR 3	WGER	2.	2.	99.	99.	2.
ACTOR 4	USA	2.	3.	3.	2.	2.
ACTOR 5	UNKM	2.	2.	99.	99.	2.
ACTOR 6	ARAB	3.	99.	2.	3.	99.

SALIENCE MATRIX

		SIGN	MBFR	ISRA	ARMS	EURO
ACTOR 1	FNCE	3.	2.	2.	2.	3.
ACTOR 2	MNCS	3.	99.	99.	99.	99.
ACTOR 3	WGER	2.	3.	99.	99.	3.
ACTOR 4	USA	3.	2.	3.	2.	1.
ACTOR 5	UNKM	2.	2.	99.	99.	3.
ACTOR 6	ARAB	3.	99.	3.	3.	99.

ON THE POLICY OUTPUT SIGN

THE OUTPUT ACTOR'S ESTIMATED ISSUE POSITION IS: -1.

CONTRIBUTING TO THIS DECISION THE INFLUENCE OF EACH OF THE OTHER ACTORS IS:

ACTOR	DECISION RULE	REFERENCE WEIGHT	STARTING ISSUE POSITION	POWER	SALIENCE
1 FNCE	IA	1.00	-3.	3.	3.
3 WGER	CB	0.78	2.	2.	2.
5 UNKM	CB	0.78	2.	2.	2.
6 ARAB	CB	0.78	-3.	3.	3.
2 MNCS	IA	0.67	-2.	2.	3.
4 USA	CN	-0.59	3.	2.	3.

EDITED PROBE ANALYSIS

ISSUE POSITION MATRIX

	SIGN	MBFR	ISRA	ARMS	EURO
FNCE	-3.	2.	3.	3.	-1.
MNCS	-2.	99.	99.	99.	99.
WGER	3.	-3.	99.	99.	2.
USA	3.	-1.	-2.	-2.	1.
UNKM	3.	-2.	99.	99.	99.
ARAB	-3.	99.	3.	-3.	99.

POWER MATRIX

	SIGN	MBFR	ISRA	ARMS	EURO
FNCE	3.	1.	1.	3.	2.
MNCS	2.	99.	99.	99.	99.
WGER	2.	2.	99.	99.	2.
USA	2.	3.	3.	2.	2.
UNKM	2.	2.	99.	99.	2.
ARAB	2.	99.	2.	3.	99.

SALIENCE MATRIX

	SIGN	MBFR	ISRA	ARMS	EURO
FNCE	3.	2.	2.	2.	3.
MNCS	3.	99.	99.	99.	99.
WGER	2.	3.	99.	99.	3.
USA	3.	2.	3.	2.	1.
UNKM	2.	2.	99.	99.	3.
ARAB	2.	99.	3.	3.	99.

ON THE POLICY OUTPUT SIGN

THE OUTPUT ACTOR'S ESTIMATED ISSUE POSITION IS: Ø .

CONTRIBUTING TO THIS DECISION THE INFLUENCE OF EACH OF THE
OTHER ACTORS IS:

ACTOR	DECISION RULE	REFERENCE WEIGHT	STARTING ISSUE POSITION	POWER	SALIENCE
1 FNCE	IA	1.ØØ	-3.	3.	3.
3 WGER	CB	Ø.78	3.	2.	2.
5 UNKM	CB	Ø.78	3.	2.	2.
6 ARAB	CB	Ø.7Ø	-3.	2.	2.
2 MNCS	IA	Ø.67	-2.	2.	3.
4 USA	CN	-Ø.56	3.	2.	3.

List of Outputs

Total number of outputs _____

Step 1: Identify policy outputs

Output 1

‾ ‾ ‾ ‾ ‾ ‾ ‾   ‾‾‾‾‾‾‾‾‾‾‾

(abbreviation)   (full name)

Step 5: Identify reference outputs

Output 2	Output 6
‾ ‾ ‾ ‾ ‾ ‾ ‾ ‾‾‾‾‾‾‾‾	‾ ‾ ‾ ‾ ‾ ‾ ‾‾‾‾‾‾‾
(abbreviation) (full name)	(abbreviation) (full name)

Output 3	Output 7
‾ ‾ ‾ ‾ ‾ ‾ ‾ ‾‾‾‾‾‾‾‾	‾ ‾ ‾ ‾ ‾ ‾ ‾‾‾‾‾‾‾
(abbreviation) (full name)	(abbreviation) (full name)

Output 4	Output 8
‾ ‾ ‾ ‾ ‾ ‾ ‾ ‾‾‾‾‾‾‾‾	‾ ‾ ‾ ‾ ‾ ‾ ‾‾‾‾‾‾‾
(abbreviation) (full name)	(abbreviation) (full name)

Output 5	Output 9
‾ ‾ ‾ ‾ ‾ ‾ ‾ ‾‾‾‾‾‾‾‾	‾ ‾ ‾ ‾ ‾ ‾ ‾‾‾‾‾‾‾
(abbreviation) (full name)	(abbreviation) (full name)

List of Actors and Decision Rules

Total number of actors _____

Step 2: Identify output actor

        Actor 1

_ _ _ _ _ _ _ _   _____
(abbreviation)   (full name)

    Step 3: Identify reference actors   *Step 4: Choose decision rules*
               Actor 2   (IA, CN, or CB)

_ _ _ _ _ _ _ _   _____   _____
(abbreviation)   (full name)

               Actor 3

_ _ _ _ _ _ _ _   _____   _____
(abbreviation)   (full name)

               Actor 4

_ _ _ _ _ _ _ _   _____   _____
(abbreviation)   (full name)

               Actor 5

_ _ _ _ _ _ _ _   _____   _____
(abbreviation)   (full name)

ISSUE POSITION MATRIX
Policy and reference outputs

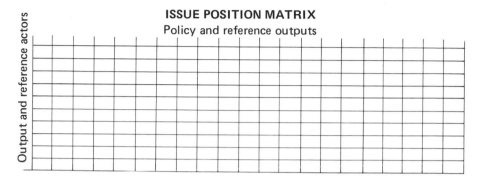

POWER MATRIX
Policy and reference outputs

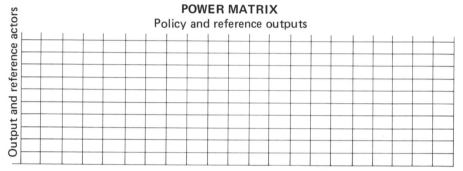

SALIENCE MATRIX
Policy and reference outputs

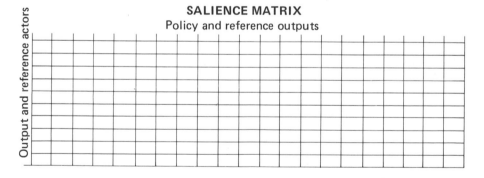

Index